PAINTING THE TOWN

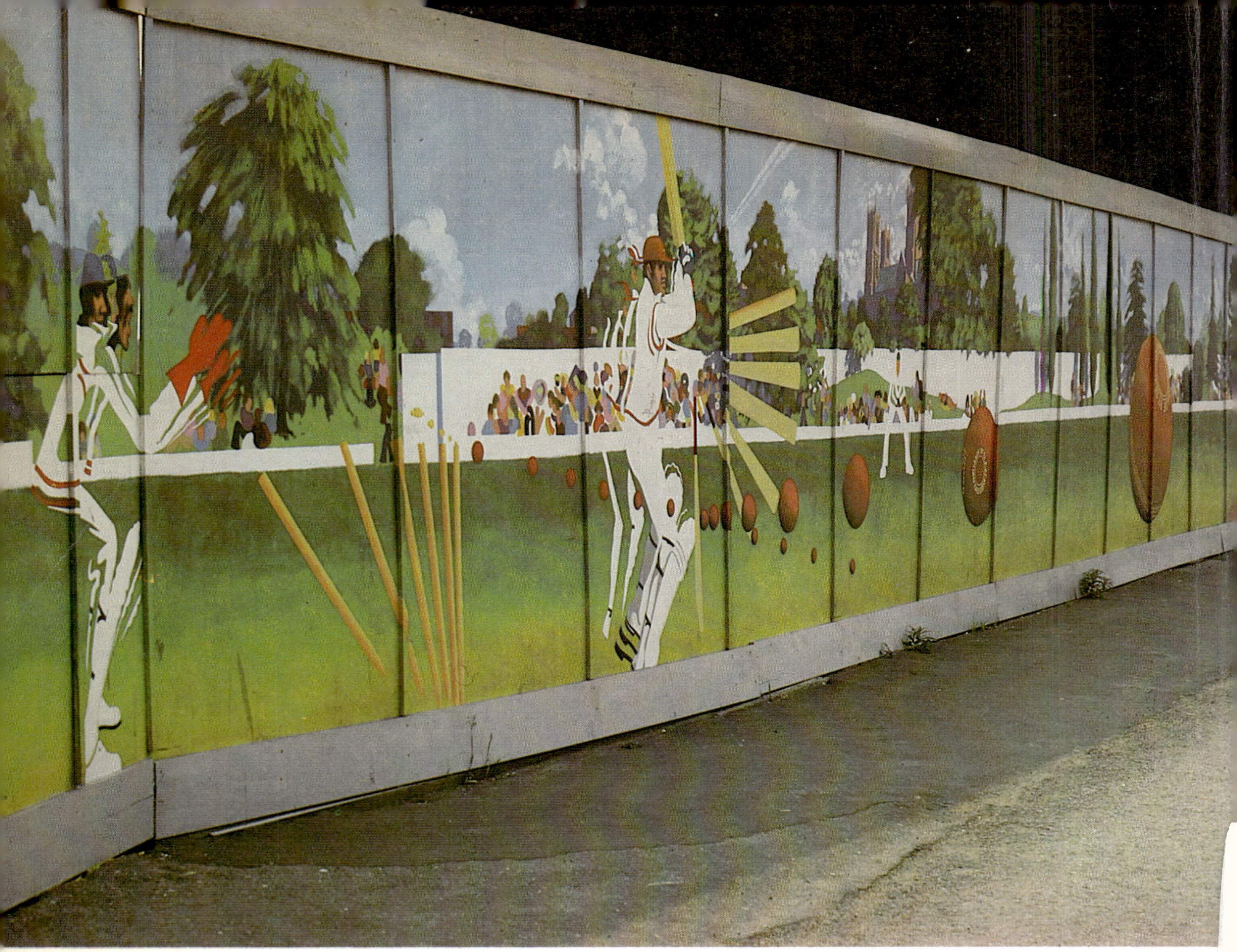

In the summer of 1976 Walter Kershaw, using gloss paints, did the whole length of this wooden fence surrounding the cricket ground in Burnley. The cricket scene, like other sections of the painting, is still untouched, despite the proximity of the local football ground.

Graham Cooper and Doug Sargent

PAINTING THE TOWN

Phaidon

Phaidon Press Limited, Littlegate House, St Ebbe's Street, Oxford

First published 1979

ISBN 0 7148 1979 4

Cover illustrations: Detail of St George killing the dragon, based on Uccello's panel, organized by the Thamesdown Community Arts Project and painted by schoolchildren *(front)*.

Spitfire mural by Walter Kershaw, Eric Kean, and a group of volunteers *(back)*.

Printed in Great Britain by Morrison & Gibb Ltd, Edinburgh

Contents

We wish to thank the Arts Council for funding the original research and for touring our exhibition, Painting the Town. We are indebted to Professor Peter de Francia and to the staff at the Royal College of Art and at the Bolton College of Art and Design. We would like to thank those close to us for the patience they have shown towards our extensive, often exhausting travels, and finally we are grateful to the muralists who have made this book possible.

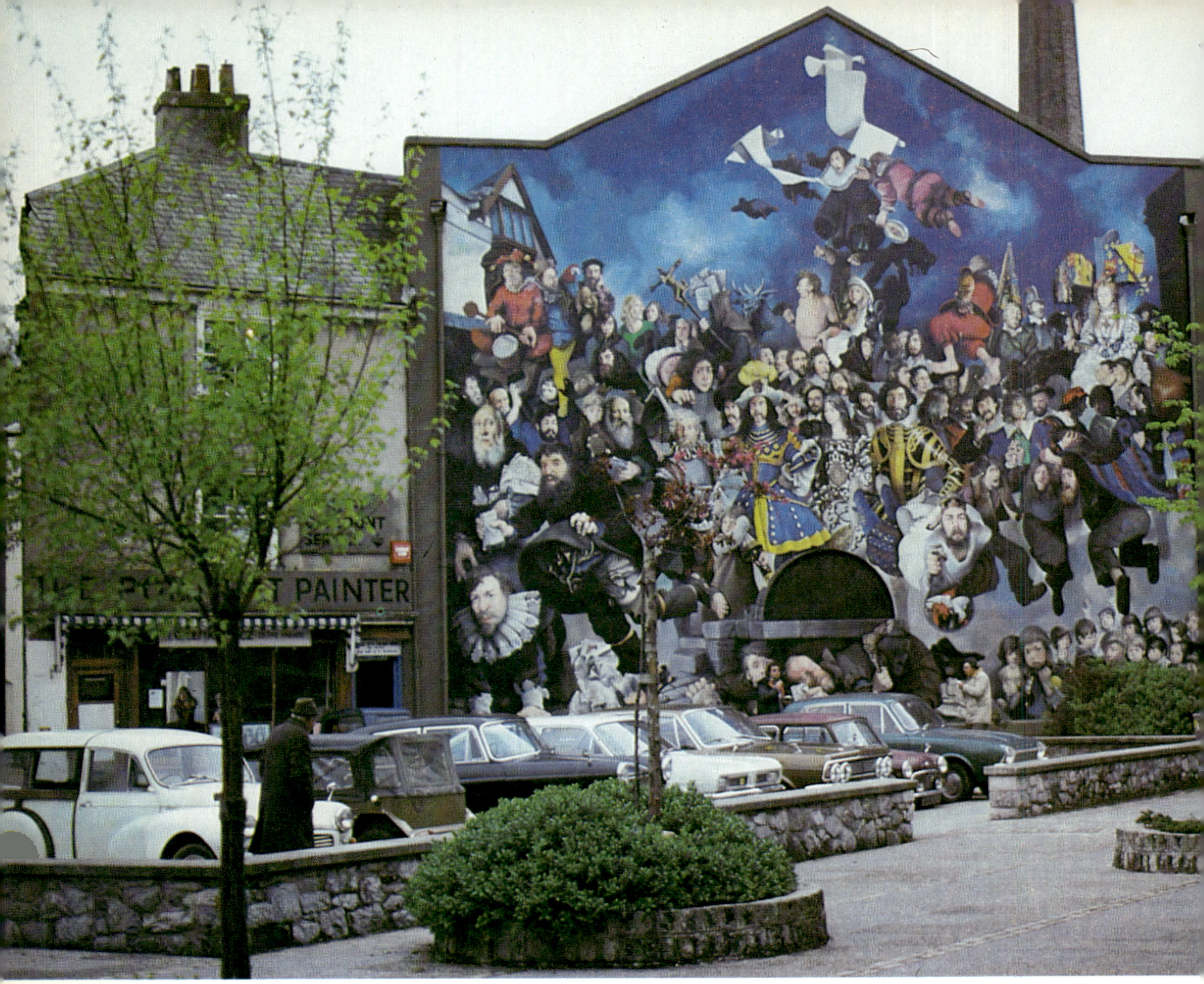

The Barbican mural in Plymouth, painted by Robert Lenkiewicz in 1972 with emulsion paints, depicts Elizabethan individuals, philosophers and scholars of the occult. It also shows the metaphysical pursuits of the time, such as alchemy, ceremonial magic, and the cult of melancholy.

The mural tradition

Murals are a practical way of brightening the environment. The reasons for painting them are numerous yet they often achieve the same result, camouflage, and break up the ugliness and drabness of built surfaces. The muralist frequently chooses the same sites as the graffiti writer; those stark, empty, lifeless expanses found on both old and newly constructed buildings. Apart from camouflaging the dreary appearance of a building, a mural can also serve to obscure its actual purpose. Reputedly the first of the recent 'big art' murals in North America, painted by John St. John in 1954, was designed to conceal a sewage-works in Miami, Florida. The *Hog Heaven* painted by Les Grimes in 1957 on a building belonging to the Clougherty Meat Packing Company, Los Angeles, disguised the real purpose of this factory by showing pigs frolicking on a farm.

Painting the exterior of buildings is as ancient a practice as building itself. In central Europe the custom of outside wall painting has survived from the Middle Ages unaffected by the specialization following the Renaissance which led in part to easel painting and to the notion of art as a commodity. Examples of exterior painting are still to be seen in the towns close to the Austro-German border such as Mittewald, Oberammergau and Innsbruck, in cities like Trento and Treviso in northern Italy and on churches in northern Rumania. In England however, painted decoration was removed from the exterior of abbeys and churches by the Reformers, and it disappeared from the streets after the Great Fire of London in 1666 when the builders were compelled to use stone and brick instead of timber.

It is believed that the central European custom of exterior painting inspired the political folklore murals that were painted in Northern Ireland from the reign of William of Orange. The tradition of painting these murals has survived through the centuries, the best existing example being the

Relief of Derry in Fountain Street, Londonderry, which is presently threatened with demolition. It was painted some fifty years ago by the neighbourhood painter and decorator, Bobbie Jackson, whose family kept this tradition alive from one generation to the next.

The origins of modern exterior murals are to be found in North America, in the outdoor paintings that emerged in the wake of pop art, graffiti, and the radical spirit of the late sixties. The psychedelic street graphics of that time gave way to more purposeful, socially inspired murals protesting against the desolation and inhuman aspects of city life. The *Wall of Respect* for example, painted in 1968 in a ghetto area of South Chicago, is an appeal to black people to remember their dignity and to fight oppression. The main contributor to this painting, William Walker, chose this medium instead of easel painting out of frustration at being rejected by art galleries. The *Wall of Respect* gave rise to a number of murals among other ethnic minorities which concentrated on issues important to their community.

Recently, murals have appeared in Britain and they are usually concentrated in the more industrial areas such as Tyne and Wear, Greater Manchester, Glasgow, Porth and Swindon. As outdoor murals are not subjected to the confines of the studio and there is such a diversity of settings, motives and traditions, an enormous variety of work exists.

The first significant modern wall painting is the Barbican mural in Plymouth, painted by Robert Lenkiewicz in 1972. The choice of imagery and consistent attention to detail suggest that this mural was inspired and carried out by the artist alone.

The most prolific muralist in this country is Walter Kershaw. Together with his friend, Eric Kean, he was responsible for a number of schemes which usually involved groups of up to a dozen assistants including local residents. While the authorities initially viewed the enterprises with suspicion, the general public supported the painters and offered them further wall surfaces. Kershaw's latest achievements, unlike the earlier works, have been designed and painted mainly by himself, without community participation.

There are two approaches to mural painting: it can be the work of an individual or the product of a group, involving collaboration among artists, community organizations or non-trained assistants working with an artist as the catalyst. Yet, whichever approach is adopted public murals do not have to justify the whims of the gallery proprietor. Good or bad, they exist in their own right, attracting the continual passing glance. They are not transferred between exhibitions as commodities in the hope of a sale. Usually commissioned, outdoor mural art has uncovered a number of new funding sources providing jobs and money which the full time artist so desperately needs for his survival.

Overleaf

above: This striking image, based on Uccello's panel in the National Gallery, of St. George killing the dragon was the first of a series of murals organized in Swindon by the Thamesdown Community Arts Project.

below: The train roaring past the Great Western Railway Works in Swindon was painted in 1976 by the Thameside Community Arts Project with financial assistance from a local brewery. During painting, older railwaymen from the nearby Railway Village regularly advised on the details of the King class locomotive.

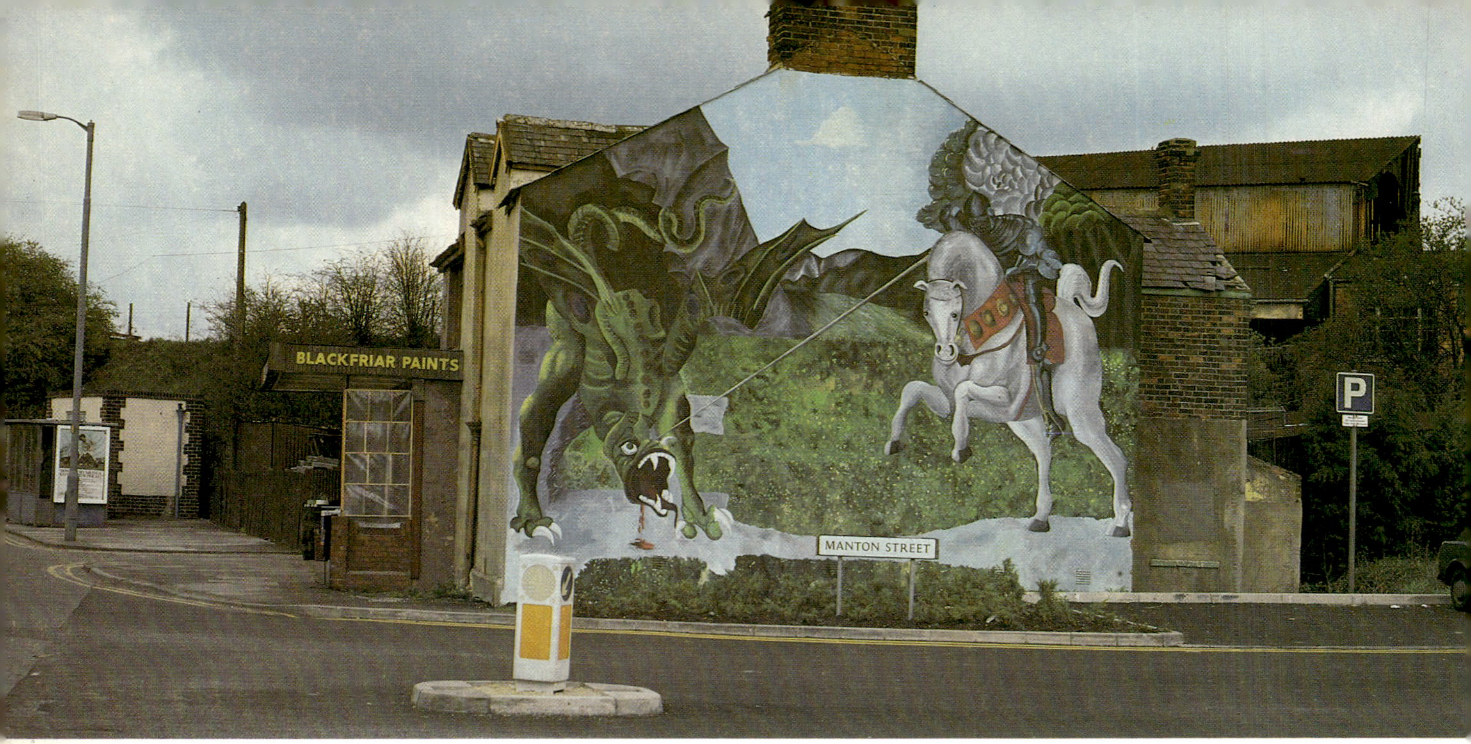
BLACKFRIAR PAINTS
MANTON STREET
P

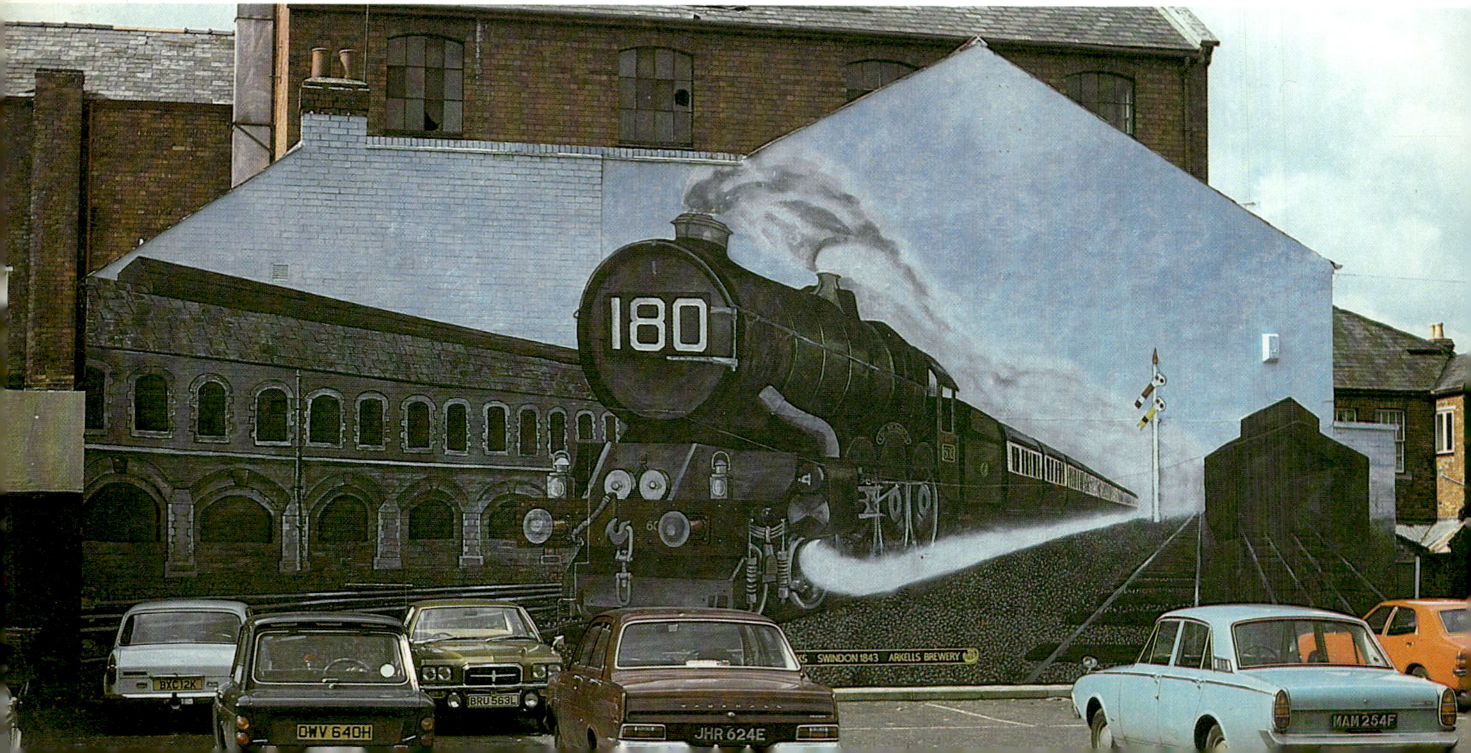
180
SWINDON 1843 ARKELLS BREWERY

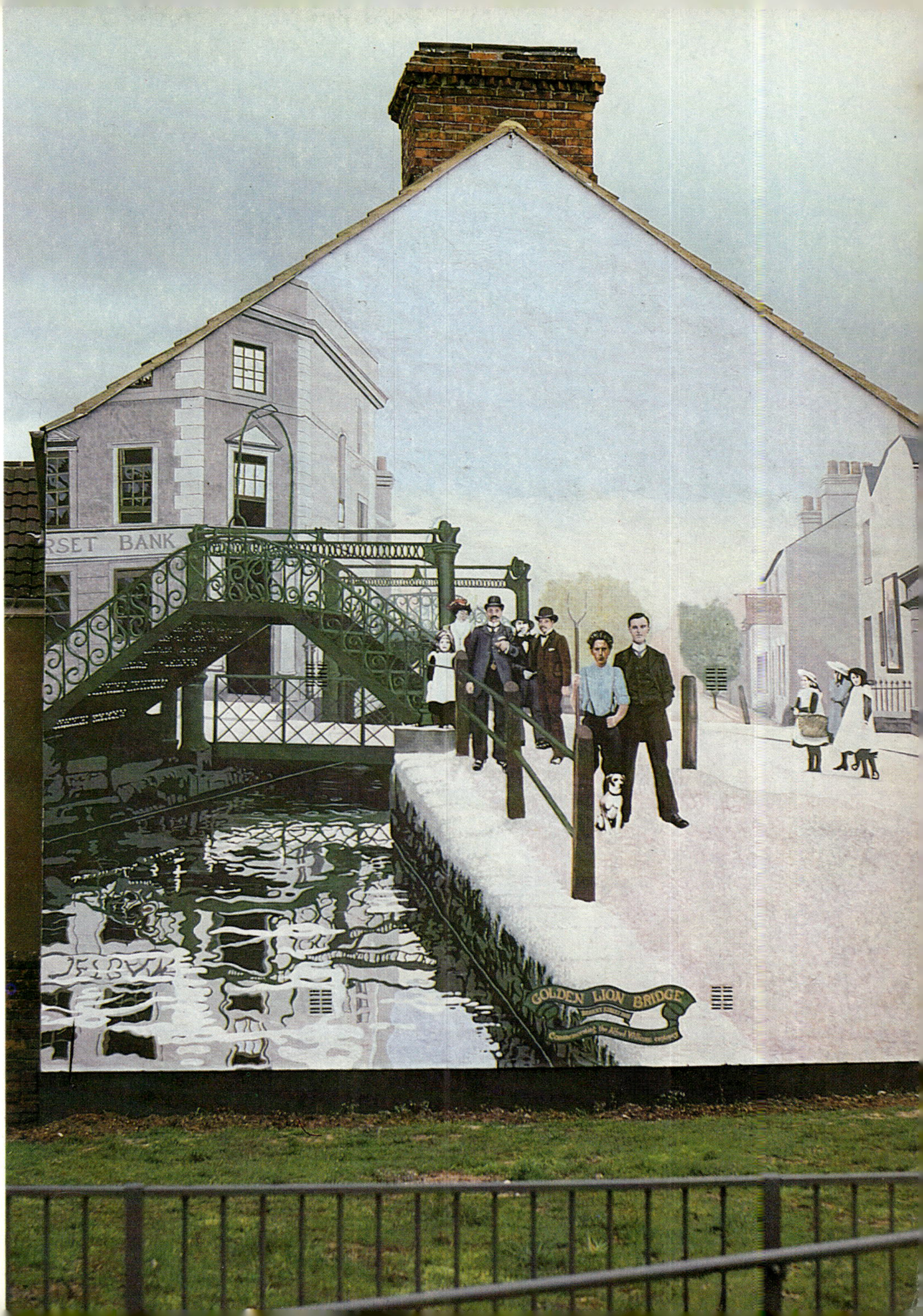

The Golden Lion Bridge mural, painted on Fleming Way, Swindon in 1976 by Ken White with the support of the Job Creation Programme, commemorates the centenary of the local poet, Alfred Williams. It also features Isambard Brunel and the now demolished canal bridge.

The first arts support organization to encourage the painting of large-scale decorations was the Scottish Arts Council. As they believed that bringing art onto the streets would brighten areas which had been ravaged by motorway planning they arranged, in 1974, a competition among the region's artists. Other authorities, like the Arts Council of Great Britain, town councils and the Job Creation Programme have since begun to aid the movement. The Inner London Education Authority funded the most researched scheme to date, the decorations of the Laycock School in Islington. The designs, based on the brick units of the walls, provide a model of how to incorporate childrens' ideas. The once dismal walls now express the vitality and self-discovery that ought to take place in every infant/primary school.

As the procedure for exterior decoration should be a 'to and fro' process between the artist, community/audience and location, limitations in the design are inevitable and necessitate some sort of compromise. Compromise does not mean over-simplification. The Laycock School scheme is the most collaborative to date, with every pupil responsible for a design and, despite the democratic compromise reached from discussions between children, staff, parents, and artists, it has provided two of the most original murals in the country. Compromise through collaboration is not a new phenomenon. History is full of groups or schools whose interacting members have been receptive and tolerant of each other and bonded by mutual interest.

It is the artist's job to provide beauty but, and here lies the difference between the muralist and the established painter, it should be set within the context of folks' lives and the total environment. Although it now lies apart from daily life, people need art. It should not be a luxury, to be indulged in or not, according to our mood or to educational and social circumstances. The artist therefore should abandon the romantic nineteenth-century attitude and integrate himself into the community and its needs.

The search for a visual language for artists emerging from an easel-painting background is very demanding. While copying styles from Mexico and North America may supply a reasonable solution, it may also provide repetitive second-rate products with which local people cannot identify. Each location has its own particular solution – which is not found by superimposing designs which were solutions to other problems in other areas. A maze of murals painted around the base of a tower block, for example, does nothing but exaggerate the height and oppression of the building. Ideally, the artwork should coincide with the initial planning of the building but at present this is unlikely with architects and planners preoccupied as they are with function and cost.

As the painting of exterior murals suggests, people are starting to react against the creative elite – made up of architects, planners and local authorities – who have been responsible for designing the environment, thereby condemning the layman to a purgatory of institutionalized drabness and homogeneity. One hopes that people responsible for the urban wastelands will take note of the ambitious attempts at exterior painting presented in this book and often painted in some of the most deprived areas of Britain. They may see in these murals the solution to many of the problems with which they are – or should be – concerned. They could set aside a small proportion of their budget so that an art project could be incorporated into the design of the building, and so help the arts move from the periphery to the core of our lives. For painting, with its power to bring to life and personalize anonymous cityscapes, is a resource too important to be left solely to galleries and museums.

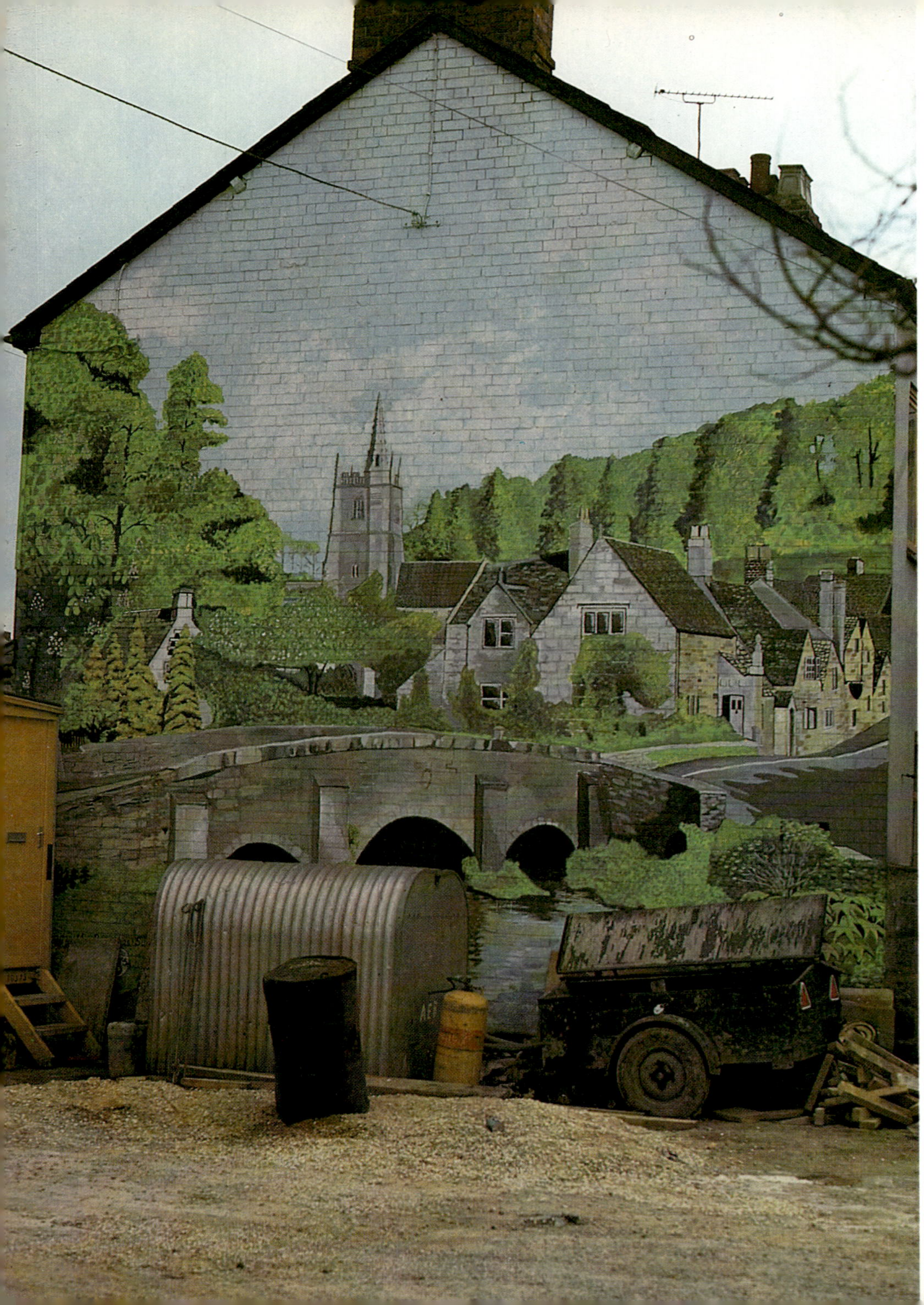

This mural of Castle Coombe presents a real-life scene in Crickland Road, Swindon. It was painted by a local scout troop with the assistance of the Thamesdown Community Arts Project.

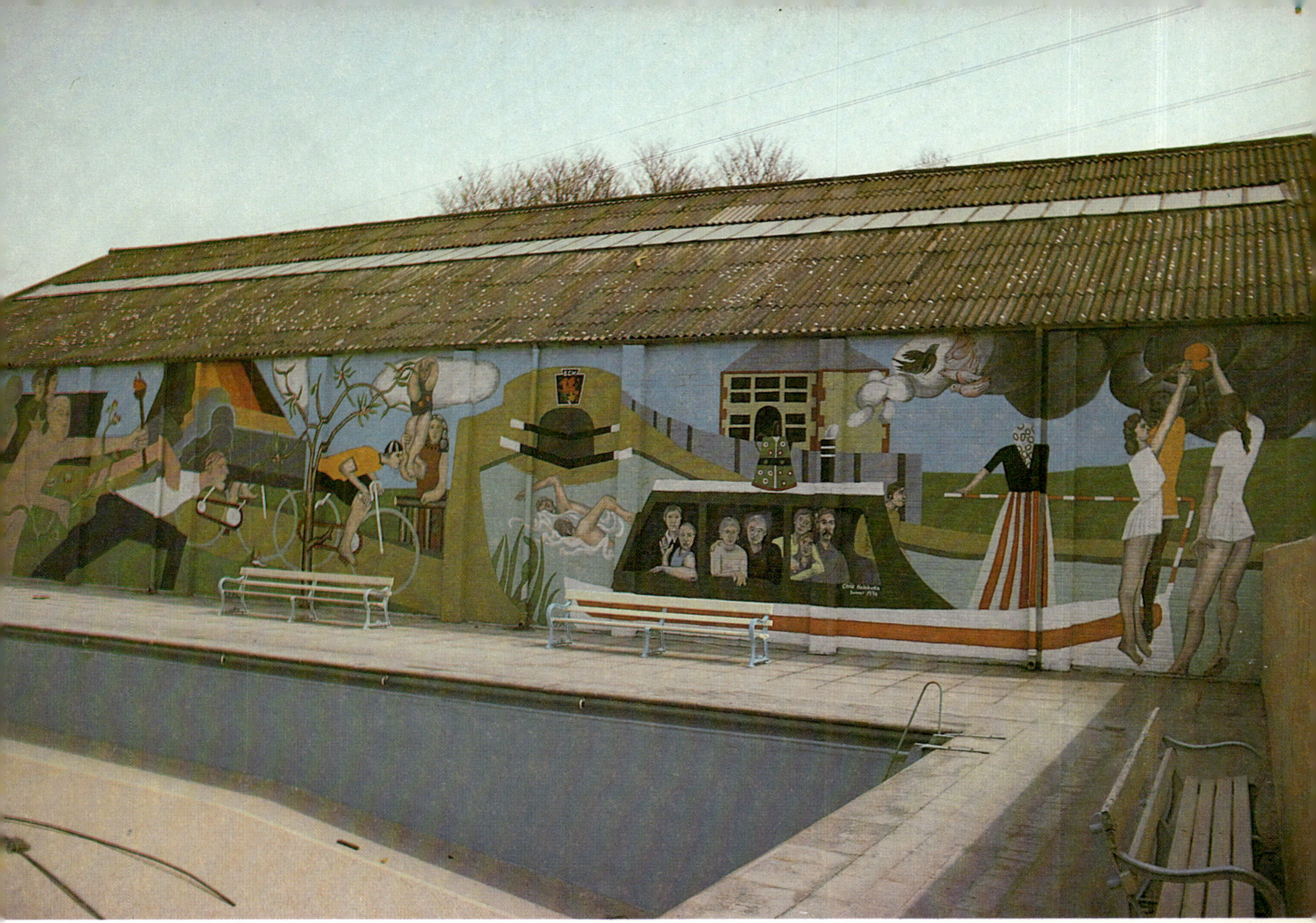

The sports shown on the mural next to the swimming pool represent the recreational facilities available at the Boys Village, Barry, a camp for boys from the Welsh valleys. It was painted in 1976 by Chris Halabula with the aid of the Job Creation Programme.

Opposite

above: There are several 'murinals' such as this one on the Aberrhondda Road, Porth. A former graffiti site, the mural now depicts the industrial heritage of the Rhondda Valley. It was painted by Alan Warburton and by children from the local comprehensive school, and was visited by Prince Charles in 1976.

below: This scene of ships at sea is painted on the Welin Davit marine engineering factory, Dudley. It was painted in 1977 by John Upton, one of the first artists to paint outside murals in Britain.

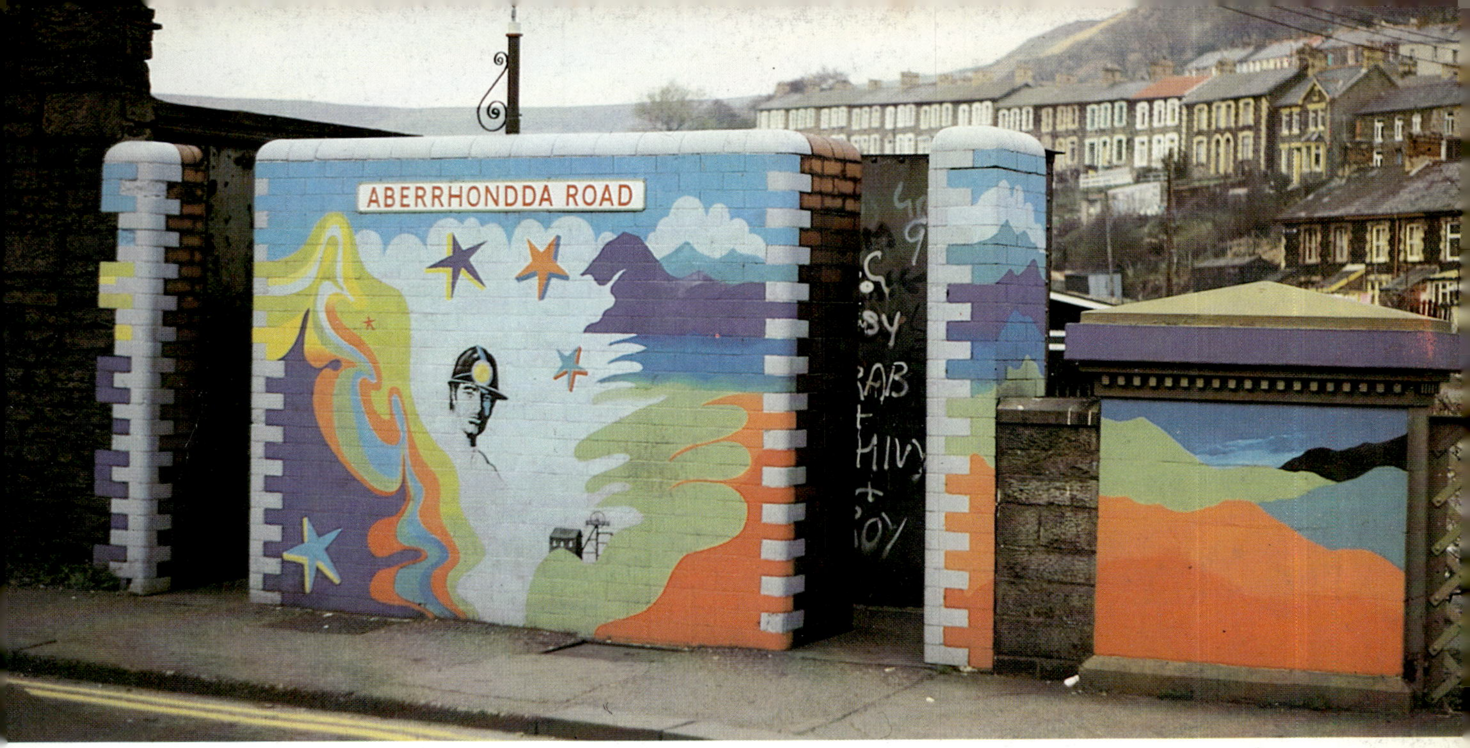
ABERRHONDDA ROAD

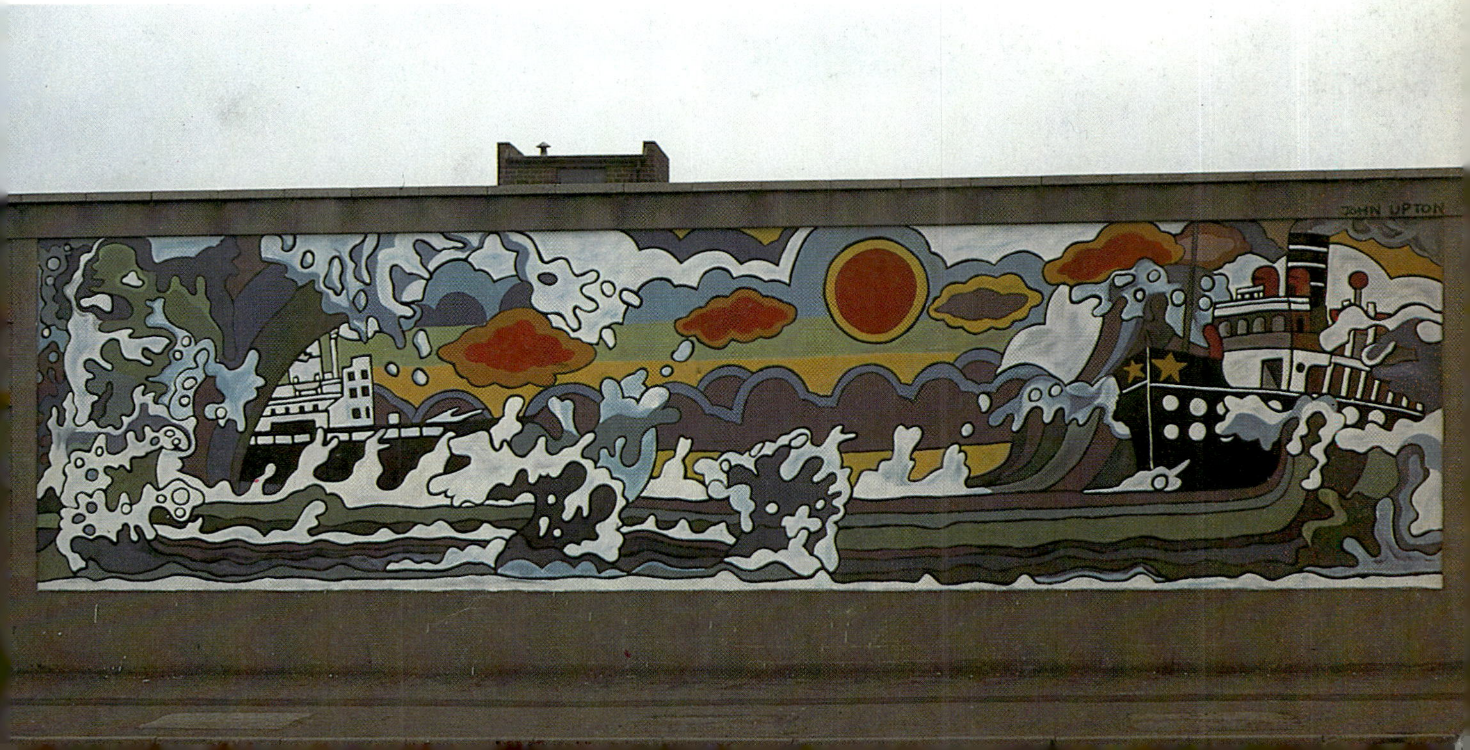
JOHN UPTON

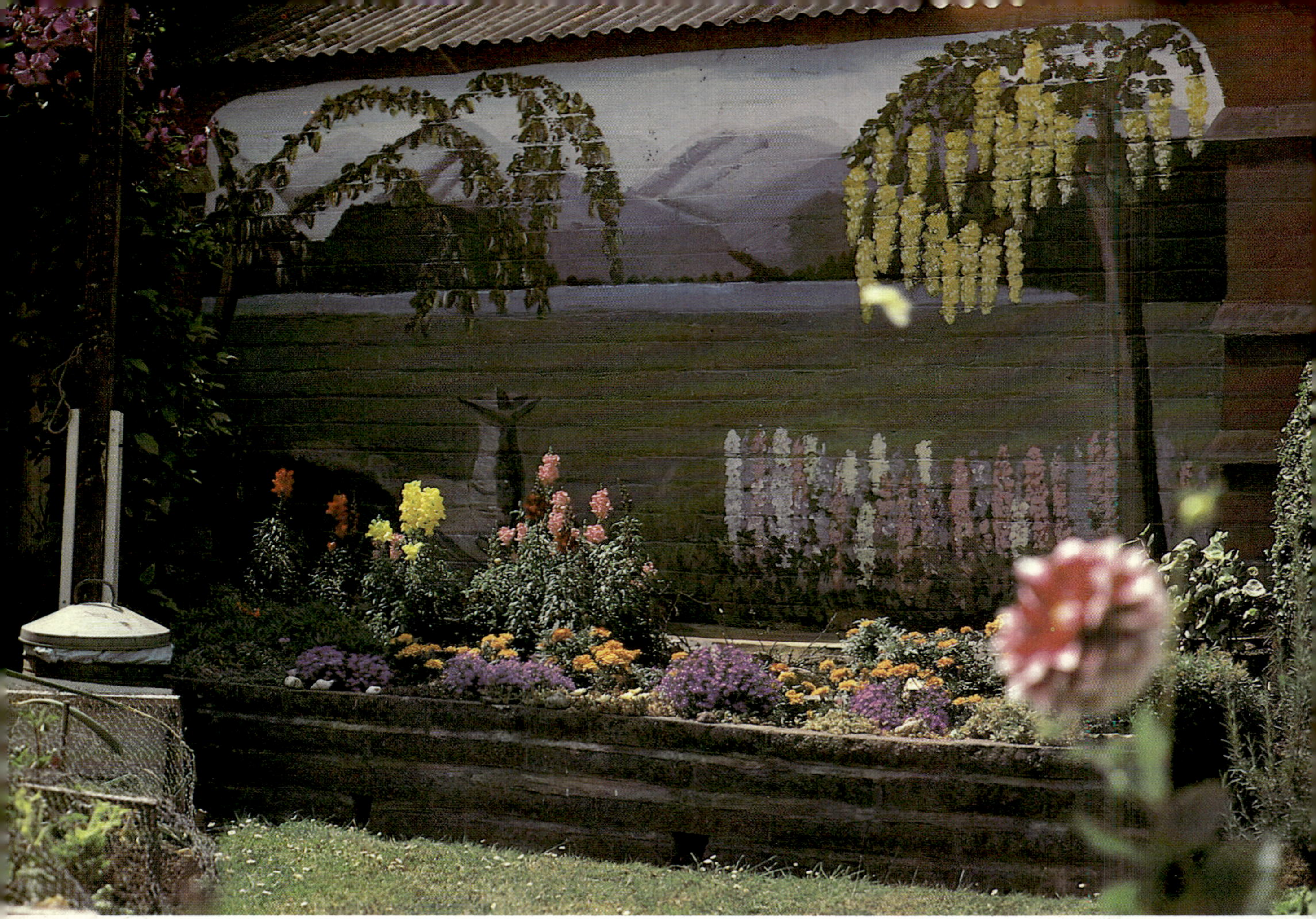

above: This garage wall, close to the living-room window of a house in Manor Way, Cardiff, was painted by the owner, Mrs G. Naldrett, to give the impression of an archway opening out on to a lakeland scene, and was inspired by holiday memories.

right: The Job Creation Programme has financed a number of external decorations including this by David Vaughan who, in the summer of 1976, supervised a team of unemployed youths on these characters from *Alice in Wonderland* painted in the market area of Ashton-under-Lyne.

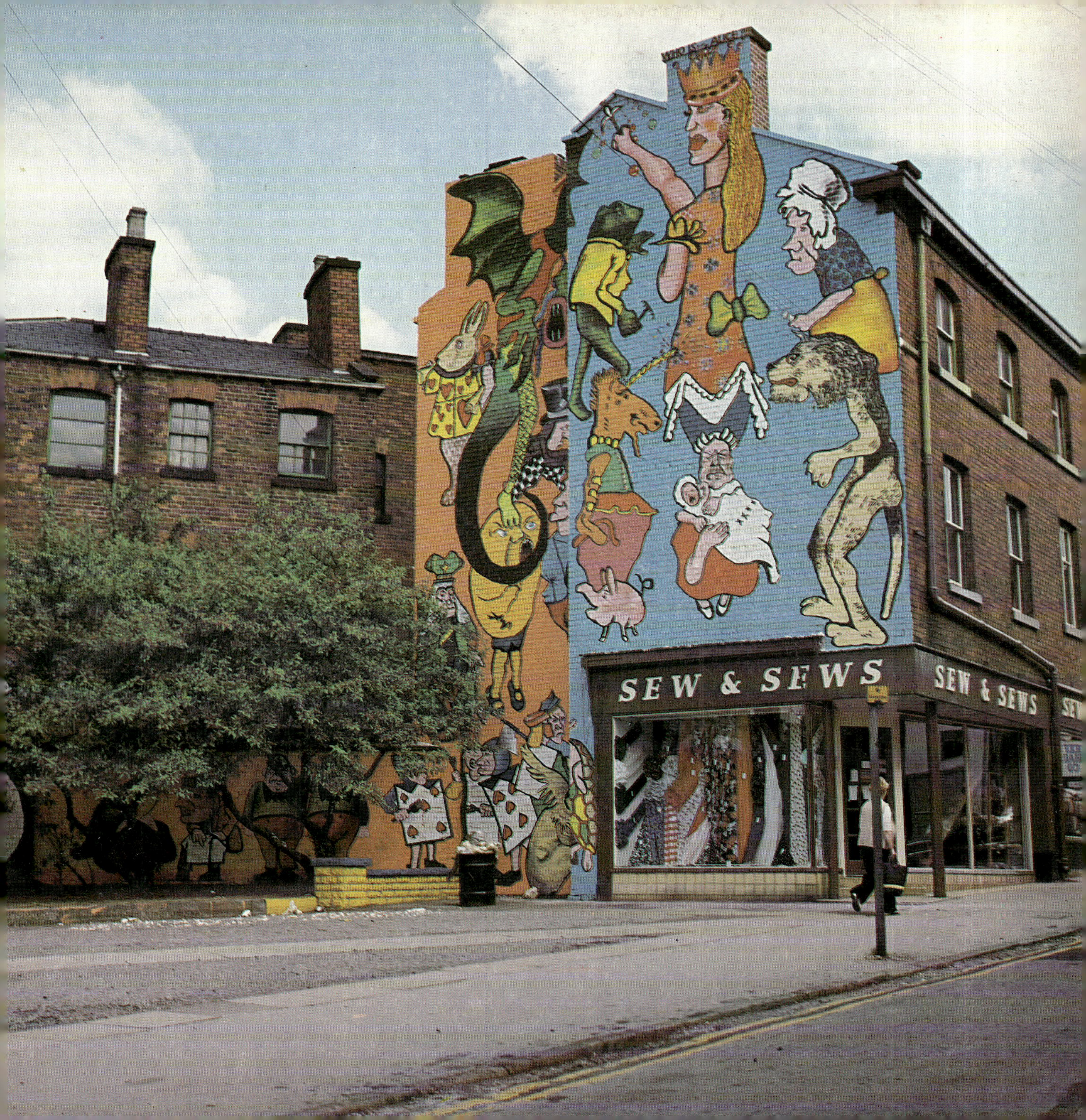
SEW & SEWS
SEW & SEWS

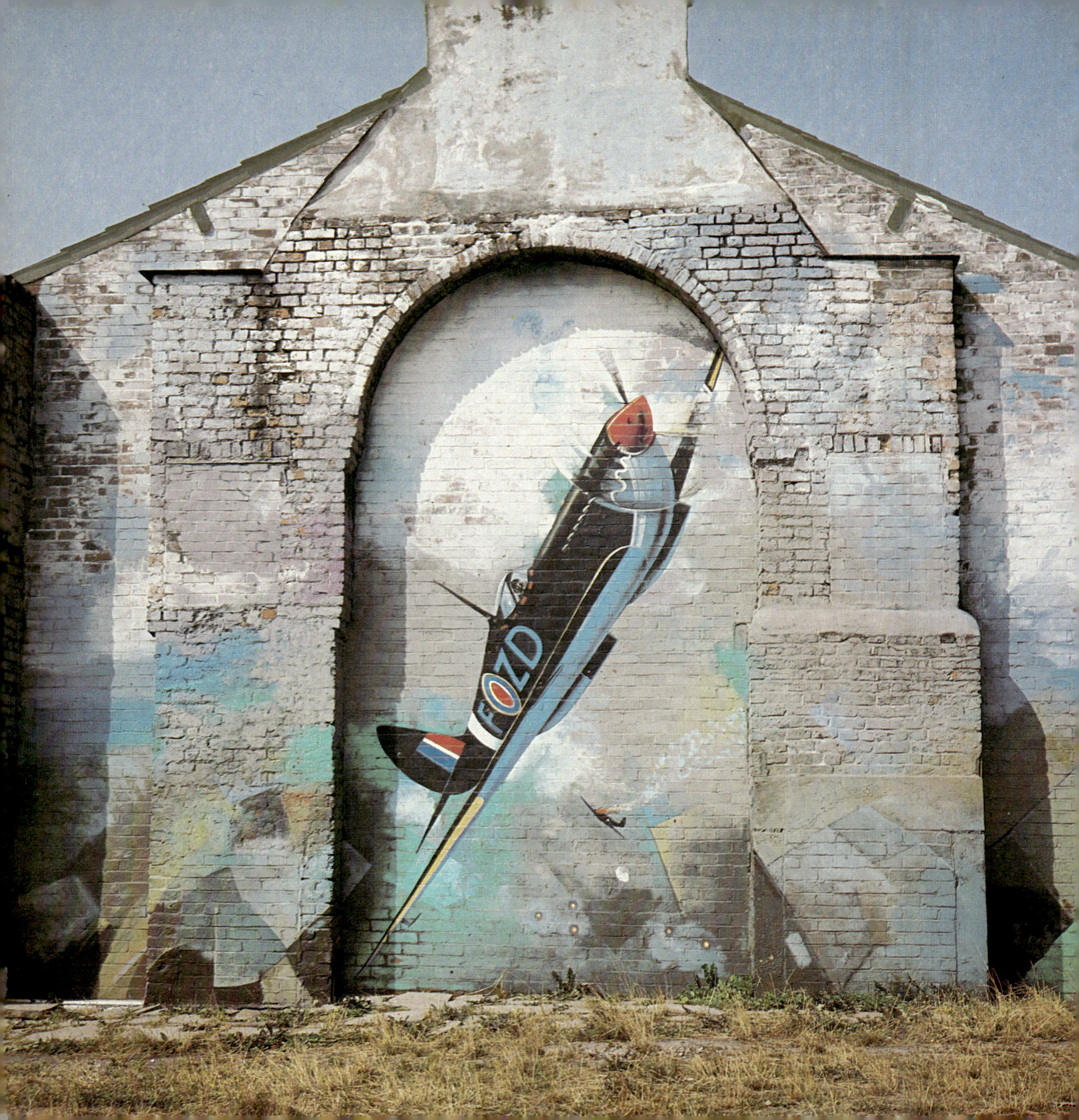
FZD

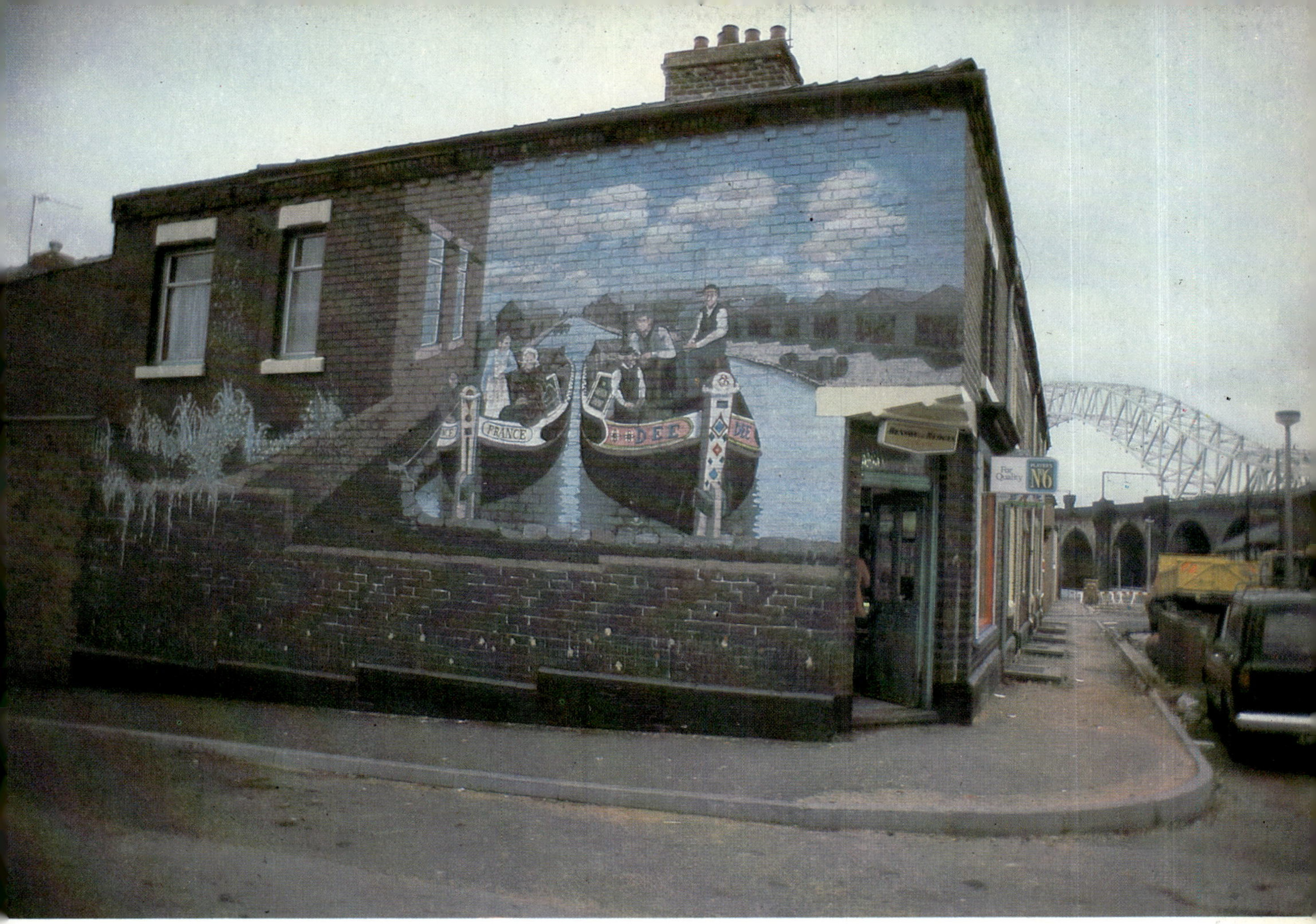

above: This mural by Pete McFerran in Portland Street, Runcorn, close to the Manchester Ship Canal, shows the narrowboats which were once so common in the area. The design integrates the adjacent windows and unpainted walls into the canal scene.

left: This mural on Peel Way, Bury, is quickly deteriorating except for the sheltered spitfire section under the chimney arch. Walter Kershaw and Eric Kean, whose R.A.F. experiences influenced the design, supervised a group of volunteers to paint this mural.

right: Walter Kershaw and Eric Kean co-operated on this mural which is now demolished but used to be in Manchester Road, Heywood. Originally, the mural was to have been of Elvis Presley but it was changed to the local pop star, Alvin Stardust.

below: Painted in 1975, this label-shaped design is one of the shop decorations done in Bangor, North Wales by Ed Povey.

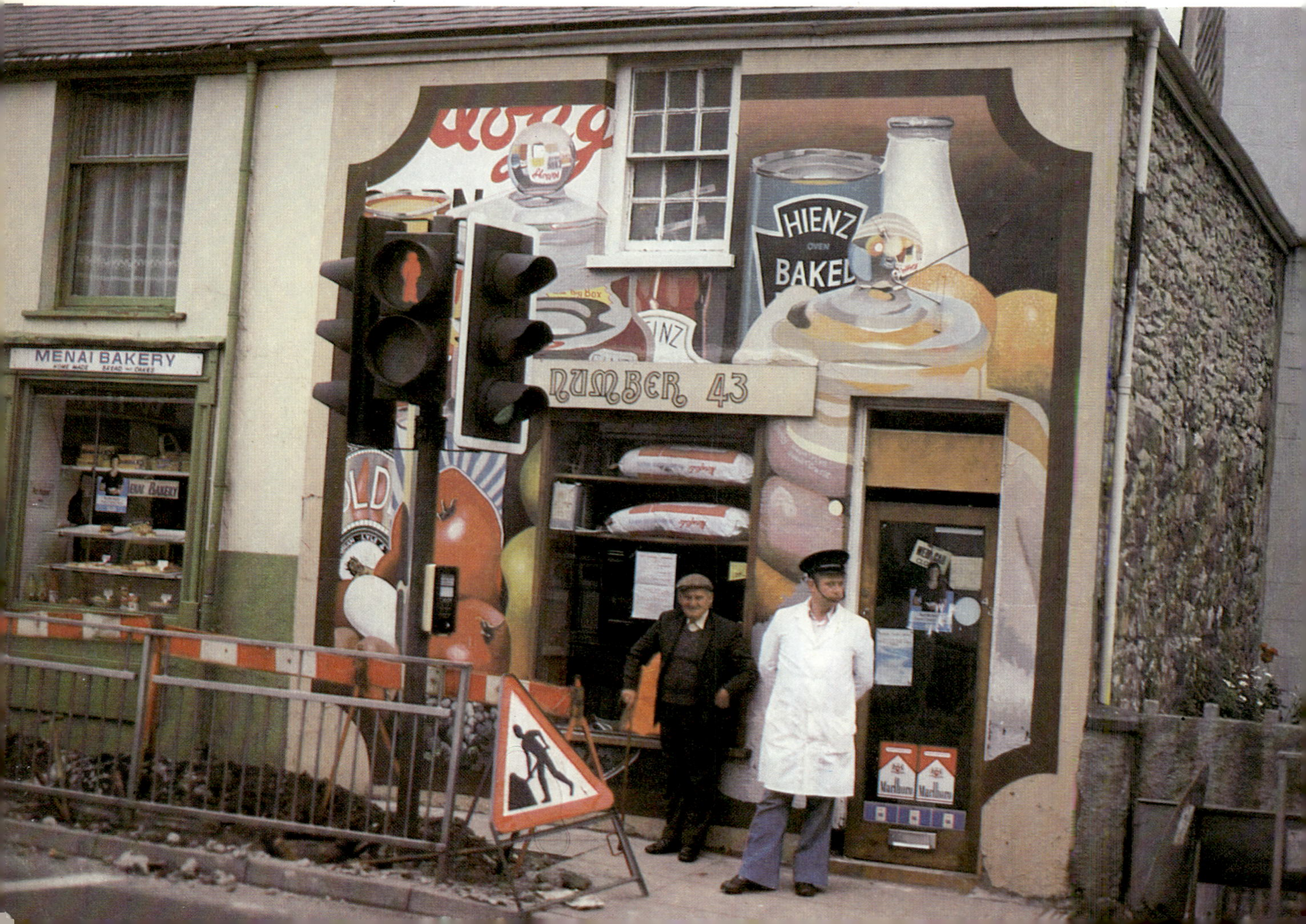

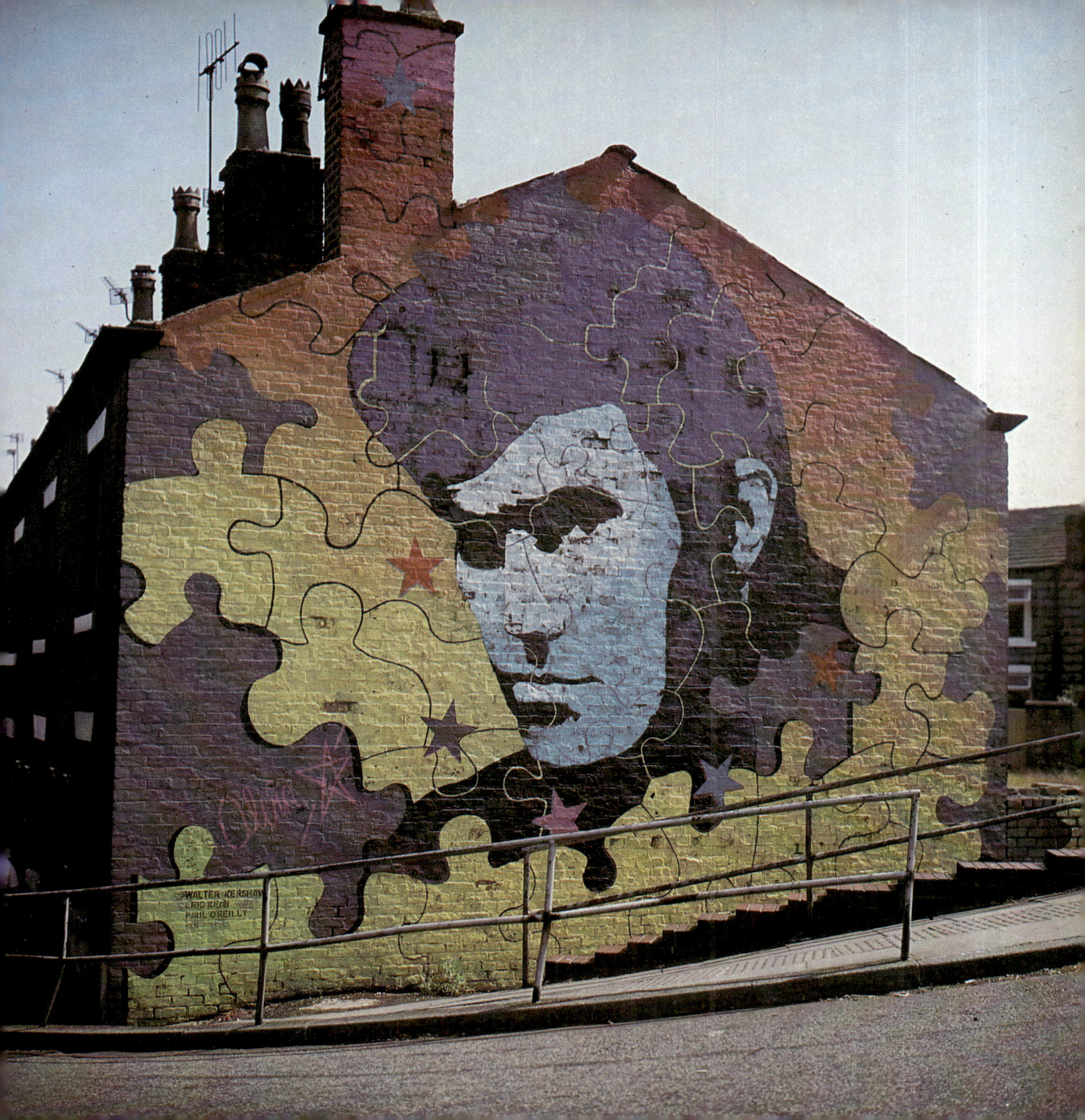
WALTER KERSHAW
ERIC KEAN
PAUL O'REILLY

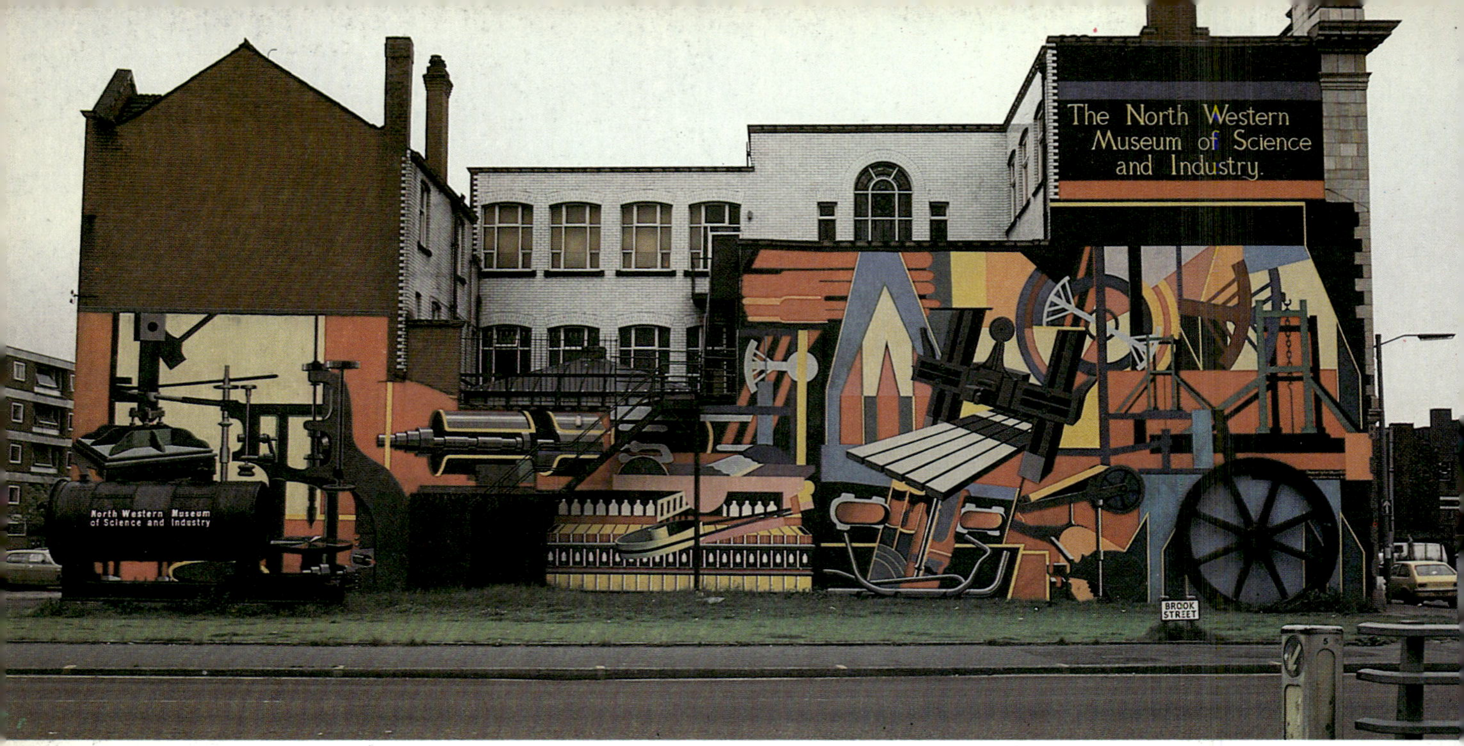
The North Western
Museum of Science
and Industry.
North Western Museum
of Science and Industry
BROOK
STREET

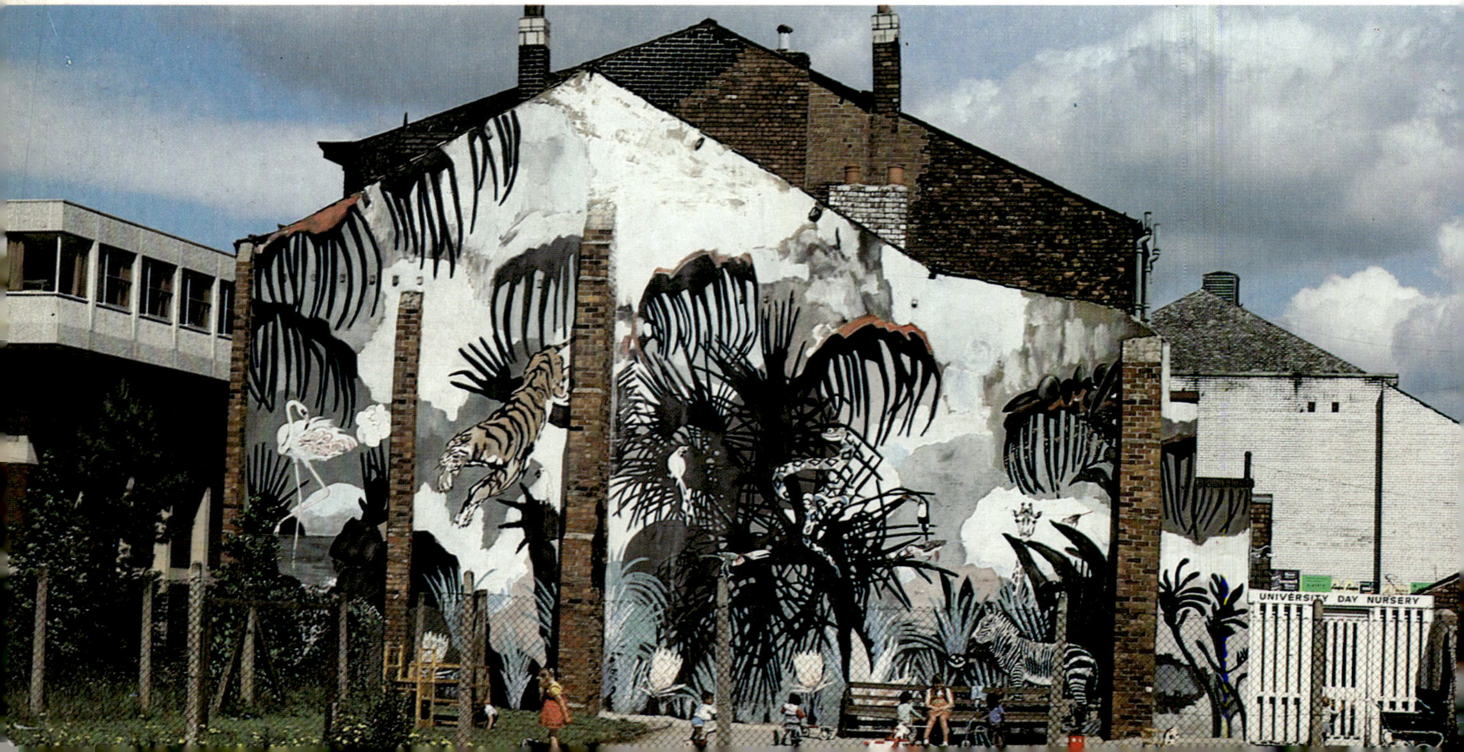
UNIVERSITY DAY NURSERY

Opposite

above: This machine mural, called *Locomotion,* on the side of a museum in Manchester, was designed by Ken Billyard and painted by Walter Kershaw after Billyard's death in 1976. The Greater Manchester Council provided the funds, materials, and equipment.

below: Glen Burton's *Tiger in the Jungle* in Oxford Road, Manchester, camouflages an exposed party wall and provides an exotic setting for a nursery playground. As this mural shows, jungle and wildlife scenes have natural rythms and shapes suitable for large scale decorations.

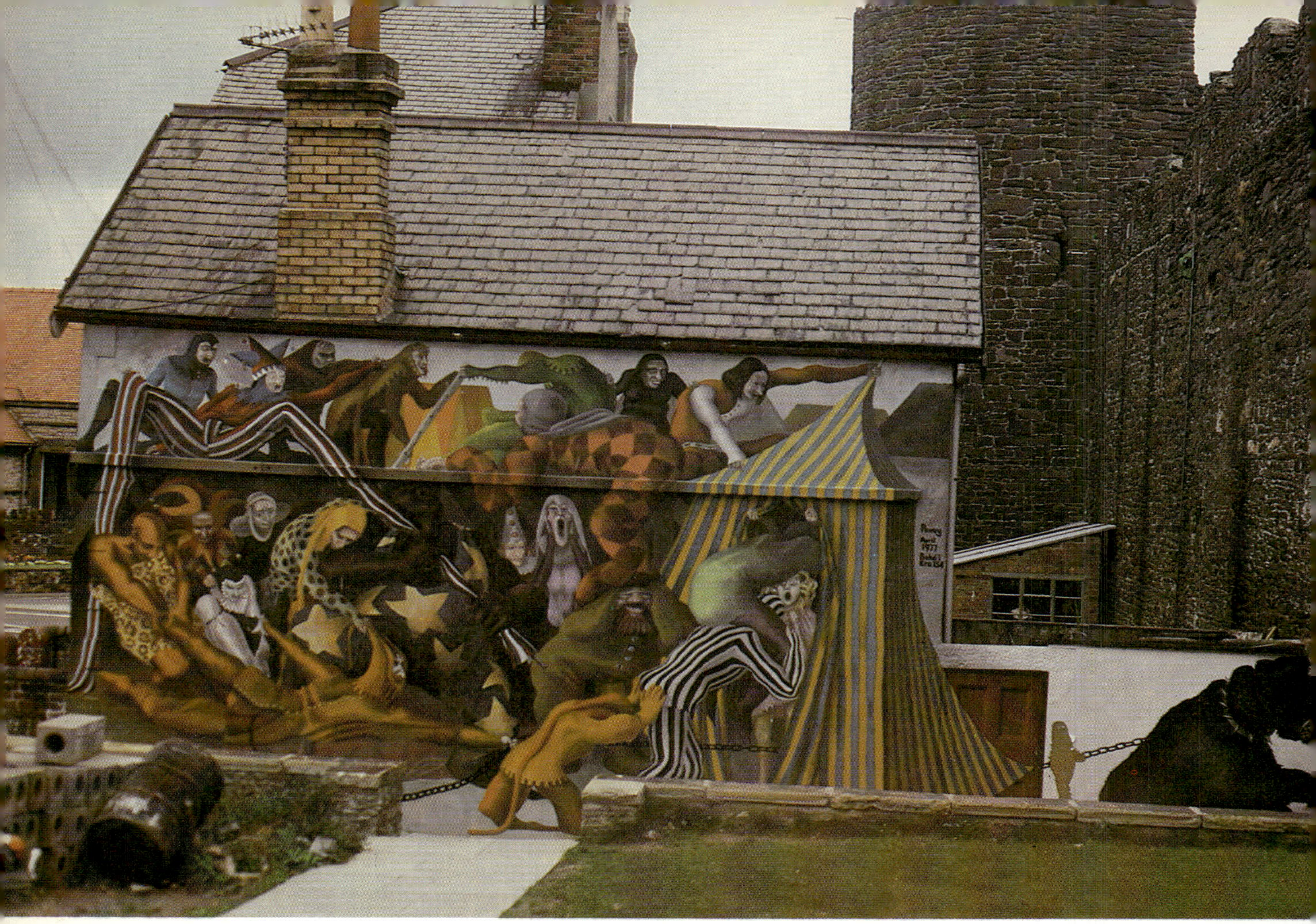

This medieval street circus scene with performers tumbling around and trying to catch an escaping bear was painted by Ed Povey in household gloss paints. Sponsored by the Aberconwy Borough Council, it is located outside the castle walls in Mount Pleasant Road, Conwy.

This mushroom cloud H-bomb mural, painted by students in Ashton-under-Lyne, is interesting in the way that it incorporates the sign post, vending machine and other street furniture into the painted scene.

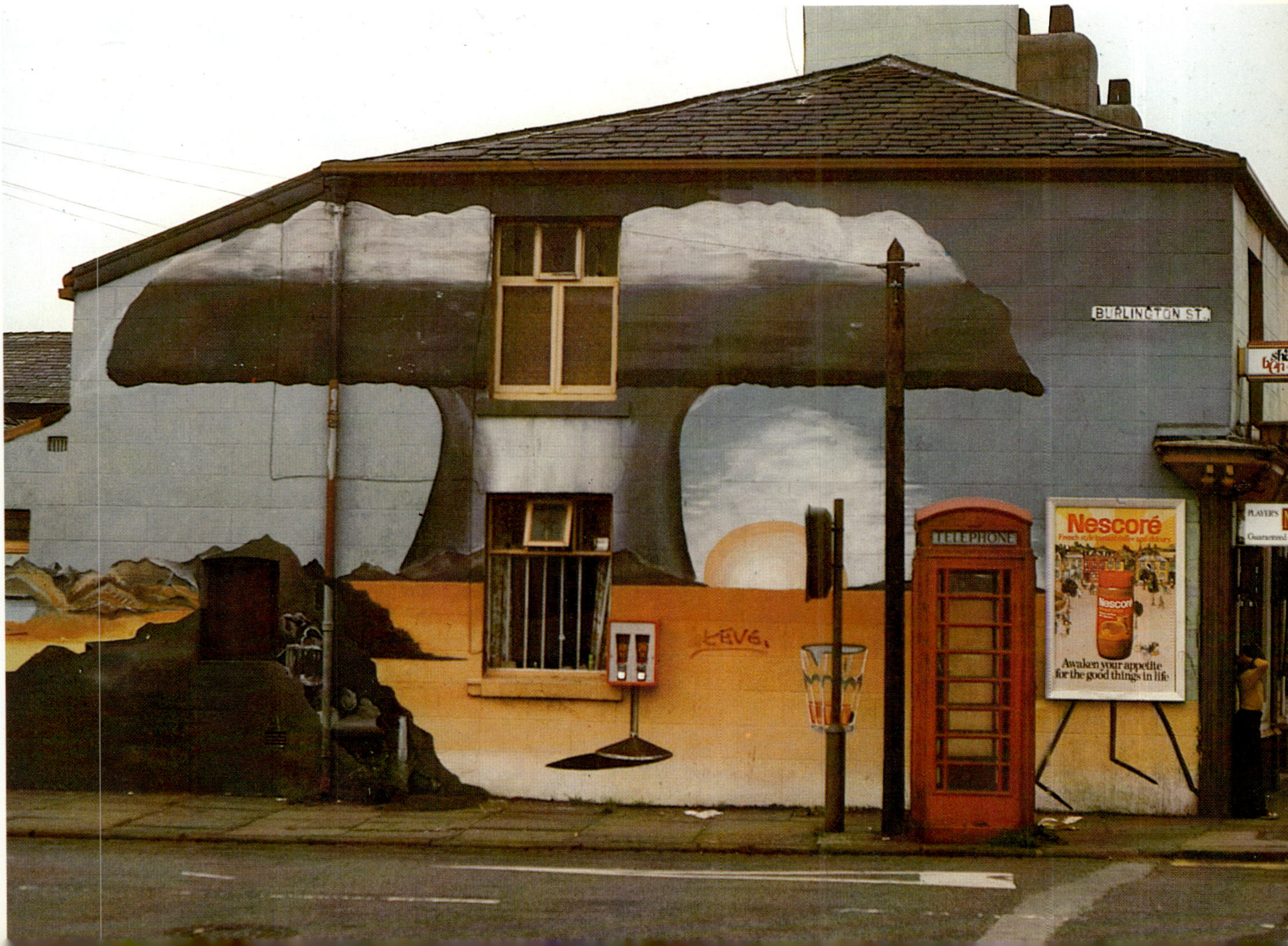

Painting a mural

Once a suitable wall is available and the issues, content or theme of the proposed mural have been agreed upon by the patron, wall-owner, neighbouring community or local planning department, the design process is ready to begin.

The dimensions and shape of the wall, as well as the atmosphere and features of the surrounding district, should be examined in detail. It is also advisable to sketch or photograph the wall from where the mural is most likely to be seen. Creating the design will probably involve discussions between the artist, workshop, community and location. It is likely that alterations to the design will be necessary, but this is preferable to lengthy adjustments to the wall painting itself.

The wall should be examined carefully as design ideas may come from architectural features such as windows, chimneys, drain pipes, and the shadows they cast. Such features can be reinforced, absorbed or optically obliterated. Corners can be eliminated by projection lines continuing around the corners relating the forms on the different planes. The surface texture and the way building materials have been laid can be exploited, as in the individually painted brick pattern on the Laycock School.

The scale of the elements or content of the picture is usually related to the viewing distance and the relative size of the wall and its background. Reducing the sizes of the picture components can increase the apparent dimensions of the wall. Enlarging or reducing various picture components can also determine importance or establish priority. Areas furthest away from the viewer may have to be enlarged to maintain a balanced composition.

The painting will be more animated and meaningful to the community if useful or informative elements, such as signposts, sundials, natural vegetation or goal posts, are incorporated into the design. This sort of

Overleaf

---

left: This Van Gogh bus shelter in Walshaw, Bury, was painted in the summer of 1975 by schoolchildren under the supervision of the author. During the following three years the shelter was vandalized, and by now Van Gogh's eye has been scrawled out and the designs scribbled upon.

right: A typical Lancashire house interior in Derby Street, Rochdale, as interpreted by Walter Kershaw and Olive Frith. The owner of the house, Mrs Schofield, is sitting in an imagined living-room watching television. The wallpaper and carpet designs are by students from the local art college.

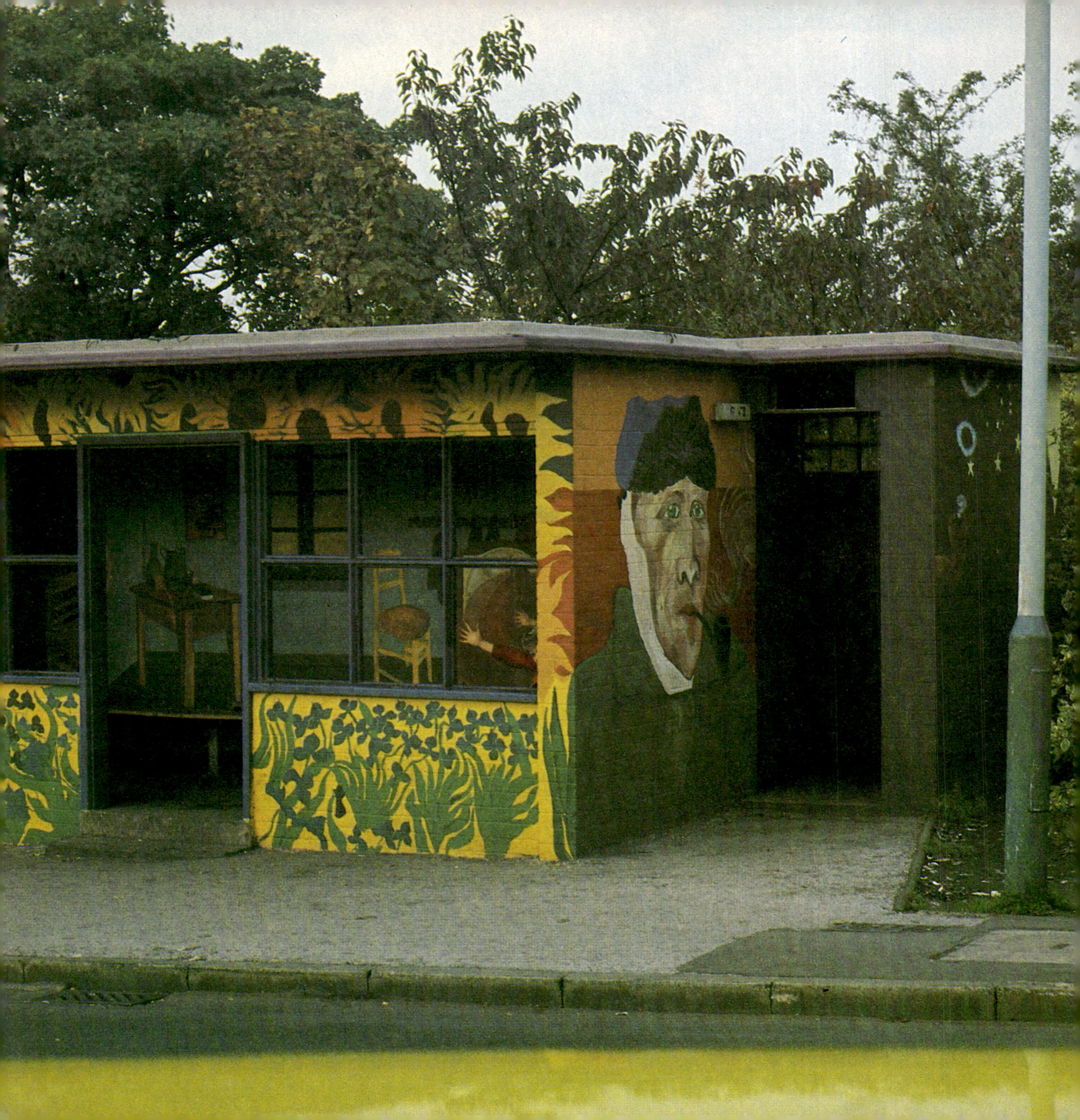

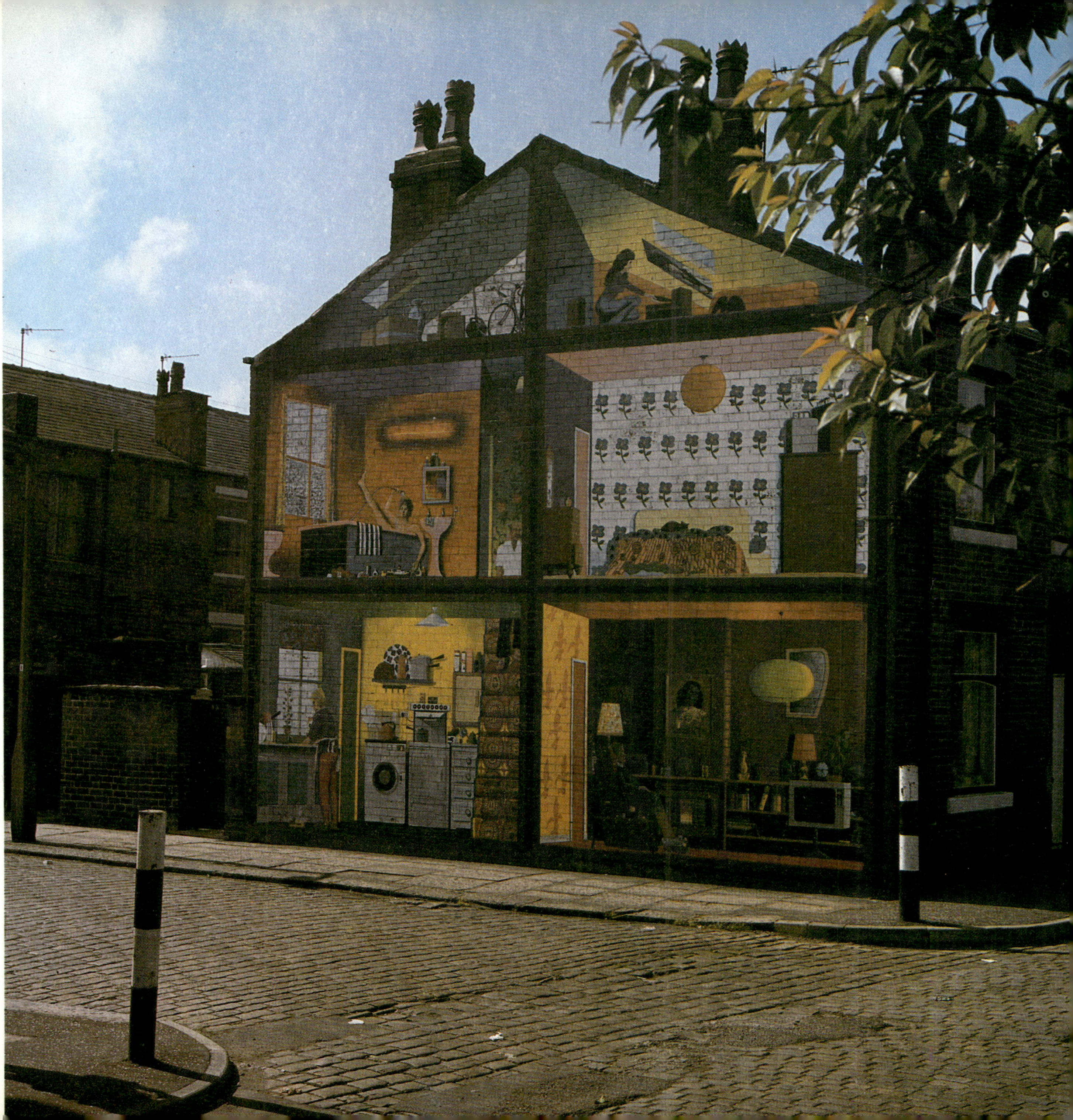

idea has been used in school playground areas for measuring, graph calculations, mazes or as exercises in letter and word recognition.

A number of decorations have introduced warm shades into cold and stark surroundings (in warm surroundings the reverse would be effective). A black or dark border around a decoration increases the apparent strength of colour. An abundance of a particular colour, especially dark or light tones on a large scale, may overwhelm detailing in another colour. White undercoats exaggerate the effect of peeling.

Once a design has been agreed upon it should be enlarged to a scale of at least 1/20 full size so that the drawing details can be included. A grid of squares should be drawn over the design so that each person involved can understand at a glance the relative position of the picture components. Large scale decorations are more manageable if stensils or repeated patterns are introduced.

The type of paint and the corresponding palette must be considered early on in the design stage. Transferring the design in one colour medium on paper to a large surface in another paint medium can alter the whole emphasis of the original composition.

Surfaces need a lot of preparation before painting can begin. No matter how good the paint, it will not adhere to damp, oily, sooty or dusty walls. Preparation for a long-lasting decoration involves time-consuming activities like scraping, brushing, re-pointing, rendering, and the removal of natural growths. The usual procedure for painting is the preparation of the surface, the application of a stabilizing solution, an undercoat or thinned first coat, two layers of paint, and, finally, the varnish.

Common problems with exterior surfaces are moisture, mould, alkali, and porosity. Moisture causes loss of adhesion, blistering and staining, so it is advisable to wait until early summer, after the wall has had time to dry out, before painting. Mould, algae, and lichen will tear the paint off the surface as they grow. They can be removed with a solution consisting

Overleaf

above: Local legend has it that Dick Turpin rode past Little Lever, Bolton, near to where Raymond Heaton painted this mural to commemorate the event. Graffiti was cleaned off regularly by the artist until his death in 1977.

below: The theme of waste being recycled is expressed in a cartoon sequence on a scrap-dealer's premises in Waterloo Street, Bolton.

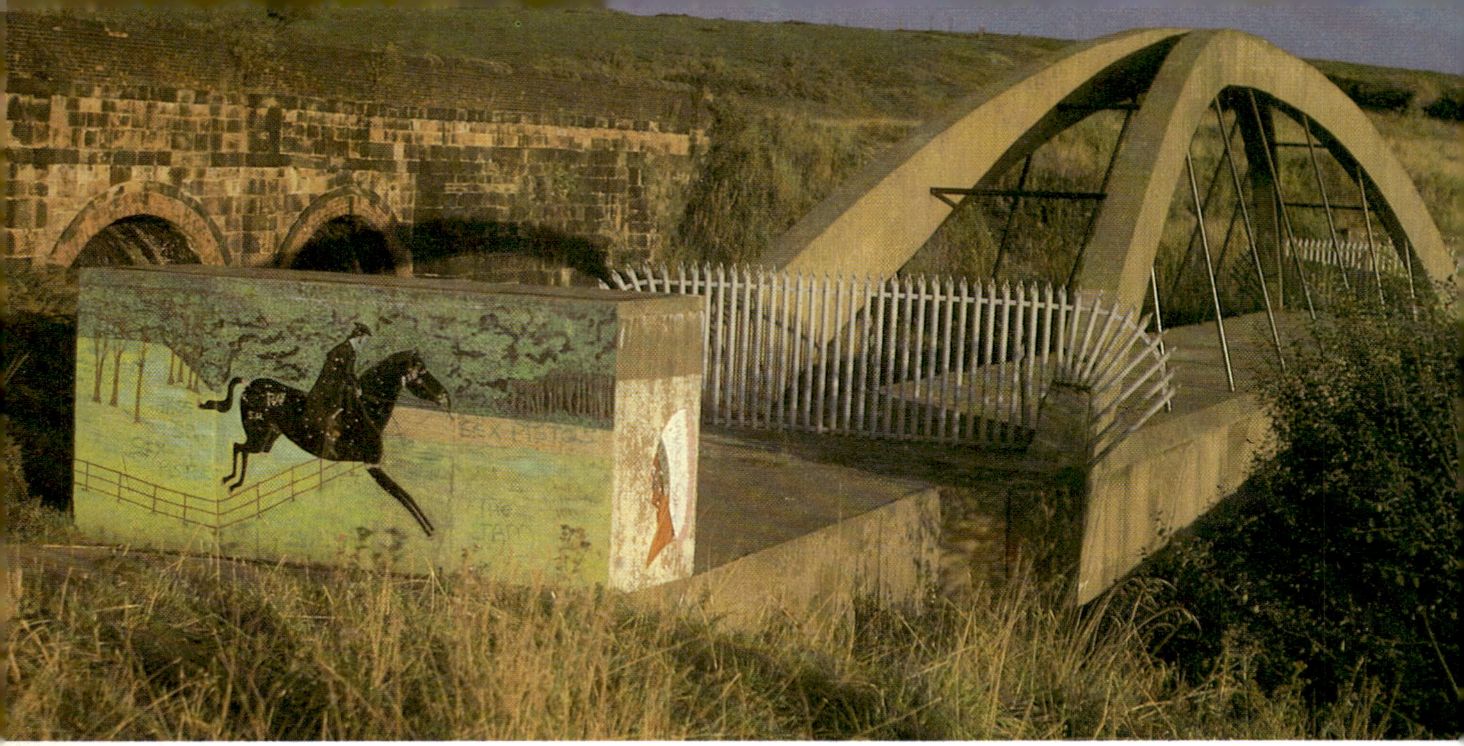

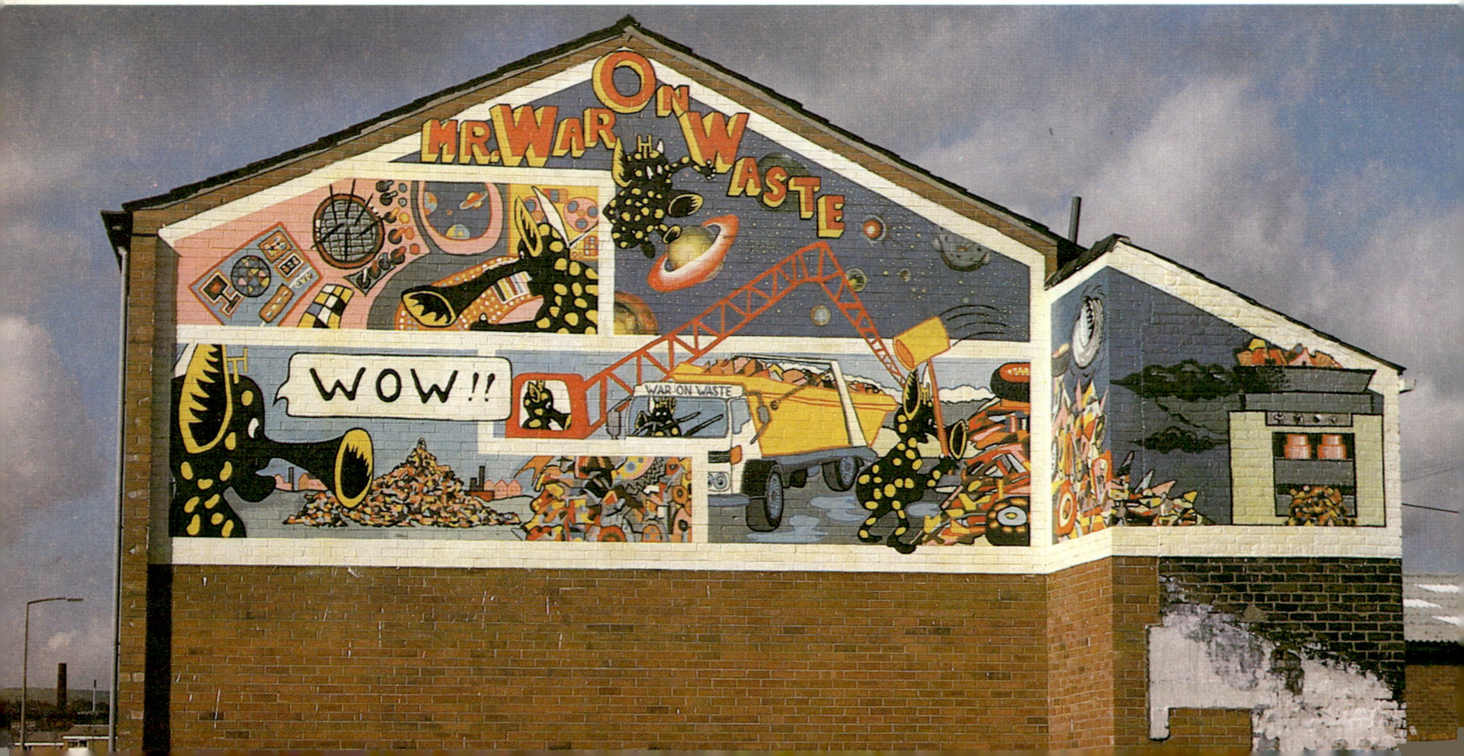
MR. WAR ON WASTE
WOW!!
WAR ON WASTE

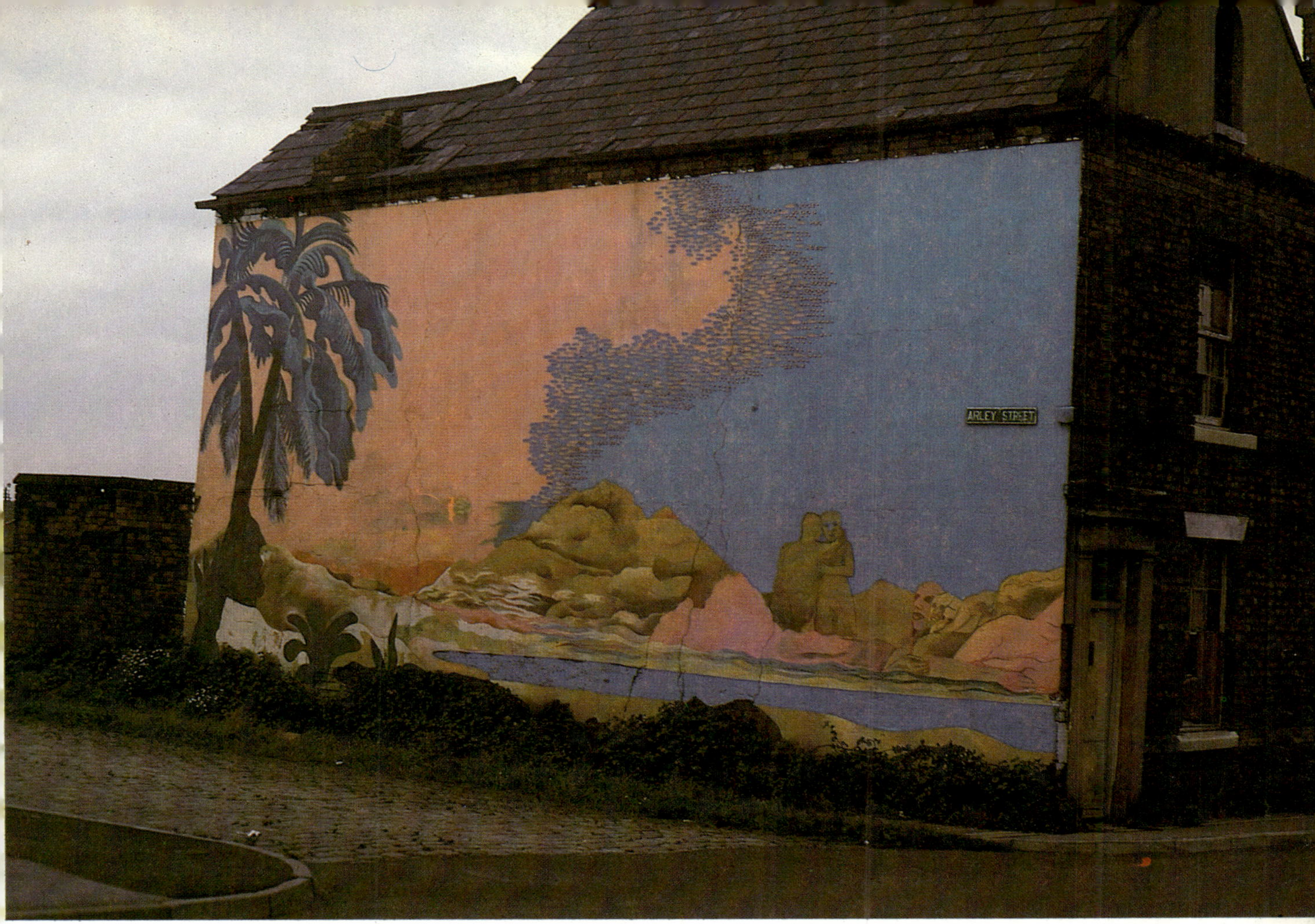

This picture of an oasis in Higher Ince, Wigan, painted by David Vaughan, aroused much local criticism. One resident wanted to know why the money spent on the painting had not been put to a better purpose, such as building a playground.

of one part bleach to eight parts water. An alkali resistant stabilizing solution can be used to seal the surface and to prevent patchiness caused by uneven surface porosity. Stabilizing solutions are primers which bind and neutralize the surface.

Most paints can be applied directly onto the wall, but the undercoat (first coat) will penetrate the surface better if it is thinned. Emulsion paints can be thinned with up to twenty-five per cent clean water, and solvent paints with ten per cent white spirits. The most popular general purpose emulsions and gloss paints have a wide colour range and are ideal for short-term decorations. On a good surface and under reasonable conditions they have a life span of three to six years. To reduce pollution and weathering effects colours with a high, light fastness, and good alkali and acid resistant qualities should be used. These colours are usually made from organic earth pigments.

The more durable exterior paints are recommended for murals which are expected to last a long time. They are however more expensive and have a limited colour range, but pigments can be added to produce a richer palette. Exterior paints usually last from five to twelve years. After this time the original surface tone and characteristics such as mortar lines, cracks, and organic growths will reappear.

Special varnishes for exterior paintwork are rare. Acrylic and solvent varnishes, and polyurethane glazes are not usually porous so that blistering and peeling occur after a few years. These common varnishes however will provide a coverage for a limited time, after which the decoration will have to be cleaned and re-varnished.

The type of paint will often depend on the wall surface. Alkali resistant paints should be used on new or recently repaired brick and stone work because of the presence of cement mortars. Strong adhesive paints such as rubber resin-based paints and gloss paints should be used on engineering, glazed or other non-porous bricks, and on iron and steel work.

Equipment will have to be bought, hired or borrowed so it should be basic but safe. Ladders, although an economical way of reaching one small area on a high surface, are not as safe as scaffolding. The angle of the ladder should be about 70° to the ground, and the user should always lean into the ladder and never overhang too far. A hook can be used to hang the paint tin from a rung so that both hands are left free. The most convenient method of access, particularly if more than one person is involved, is the roller tower type of scaffolding. Otherwise the scaffolding should be erected by experienced construction workers who can advise on safety. The height of the scaffolding must not exceed four times the base width. Ladders should not be used for extra height. Boards must be fastened to cross members and should protrude at least six inches. Permission and a licence are required from the Borough Engineer when scaffolding is erected over a pavement. Cradles and mobile automated platforms have also been used for some murals.

Painting should progress from the top downwards, so that the inevitable drip can be covered later. Splashes should be wiped away immediately with a damp cloth or sponge and drips should not be allowed to dry on clothing. Paints have to be mixed thoroughly. The amount of time that the manufacturer recommends between coats should be respected. Specific areas should not be completed down to the smallest detail while other parts are still untouched. A balance can be maintained if the whole length of the decoration is painted and evaluated at each stage. Finally, the mural is better left uncovered so that the public can monitor progress.

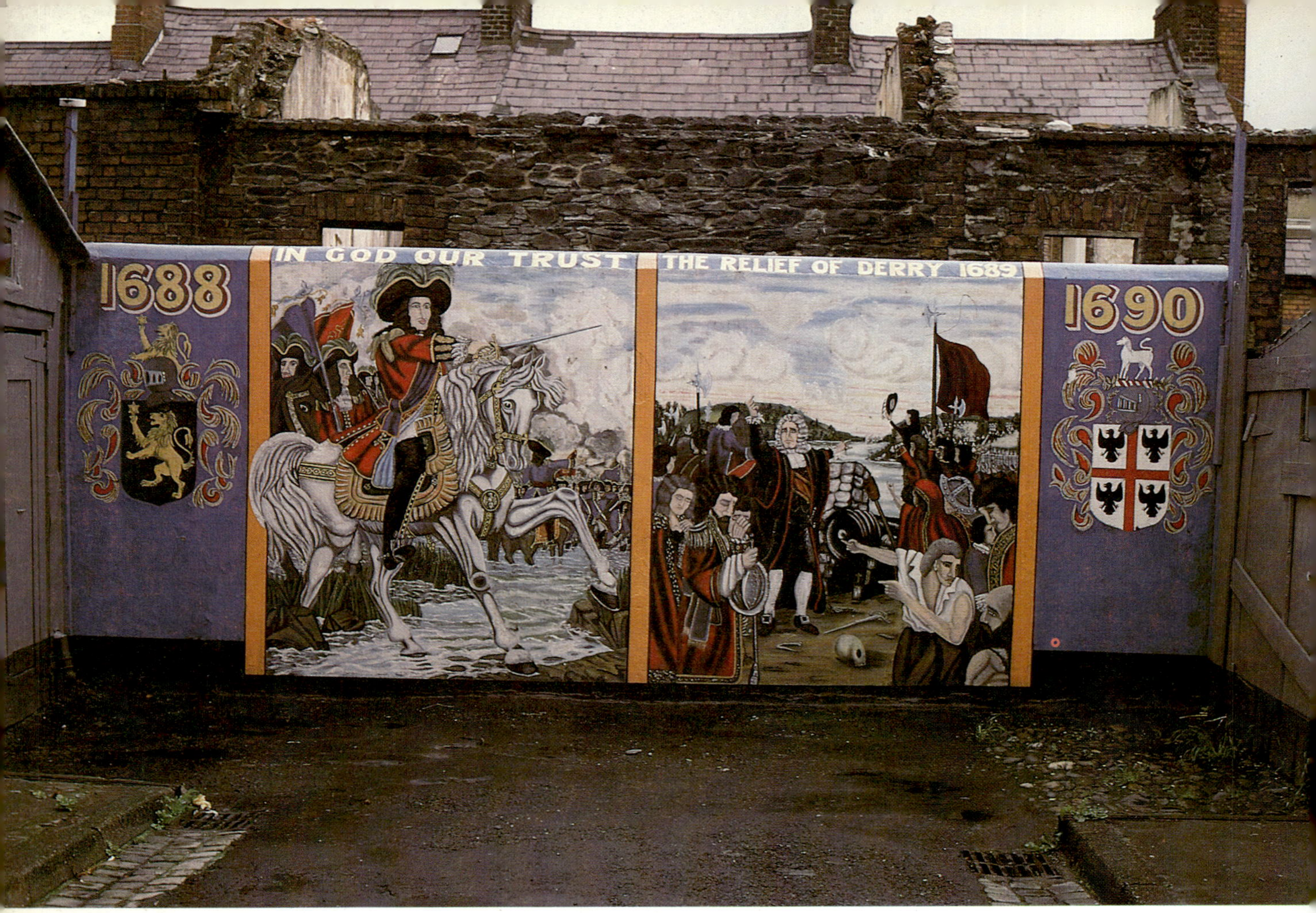

Fountain Street, by the Anglican cathedral in Londonderry, probably contained the best King Billy (William of Orange) murals in Northern Ireland. This mural is to be moved to a new location due to the demolition of the street. Painted by Bobbie Jackson, it has been retouched annually.

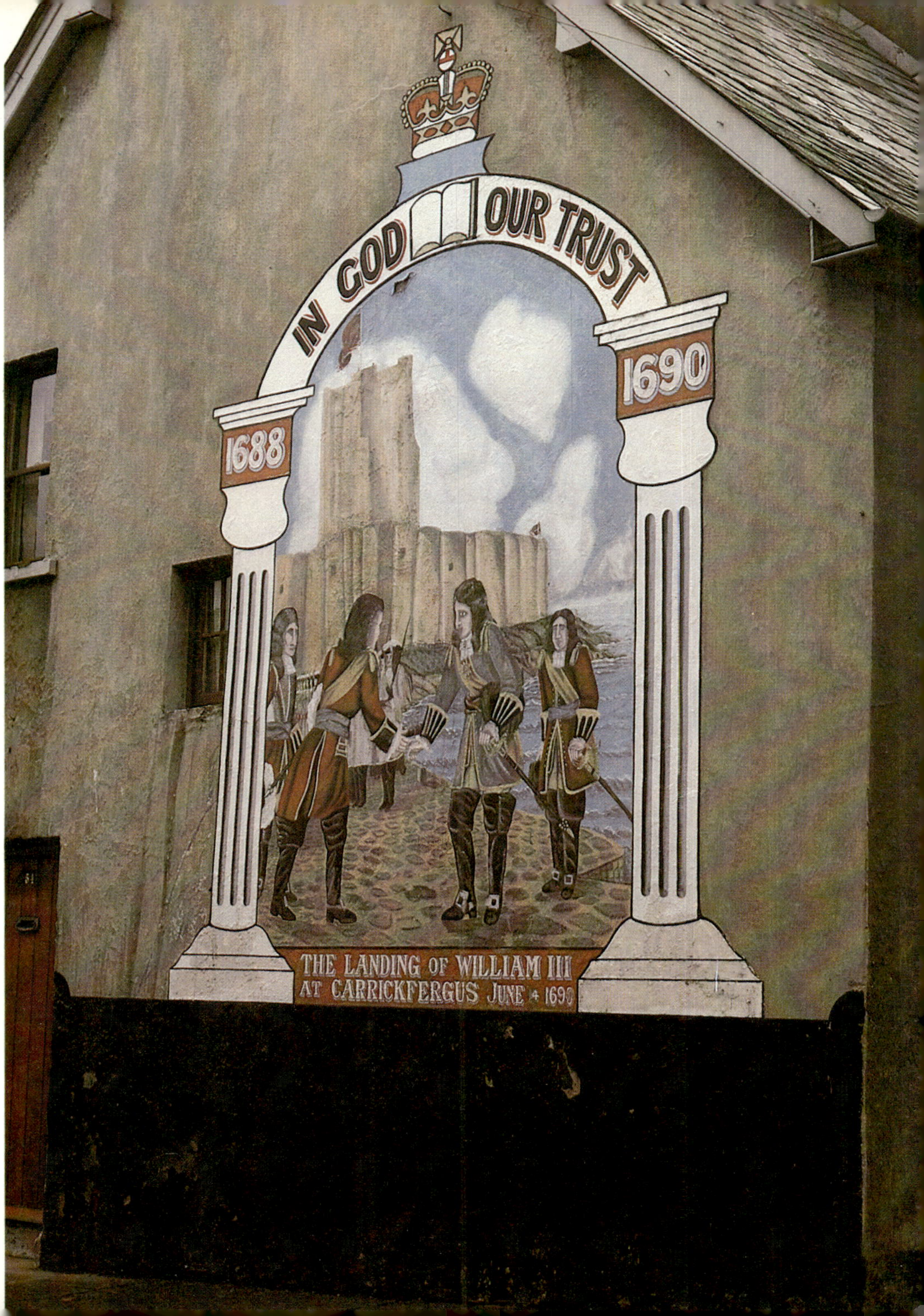

This mural depicts the landing of William of Orange. It was painted by Bobbie Jackson about fifty years ago and, like the previous example, is from Fountain Street.

Situated in Donegal Road, Belfast, this is representative of the many murals depicting the Protestant hero, William of Orange. As in early paintings, these King Billies were usually the creation of anonymous artists.

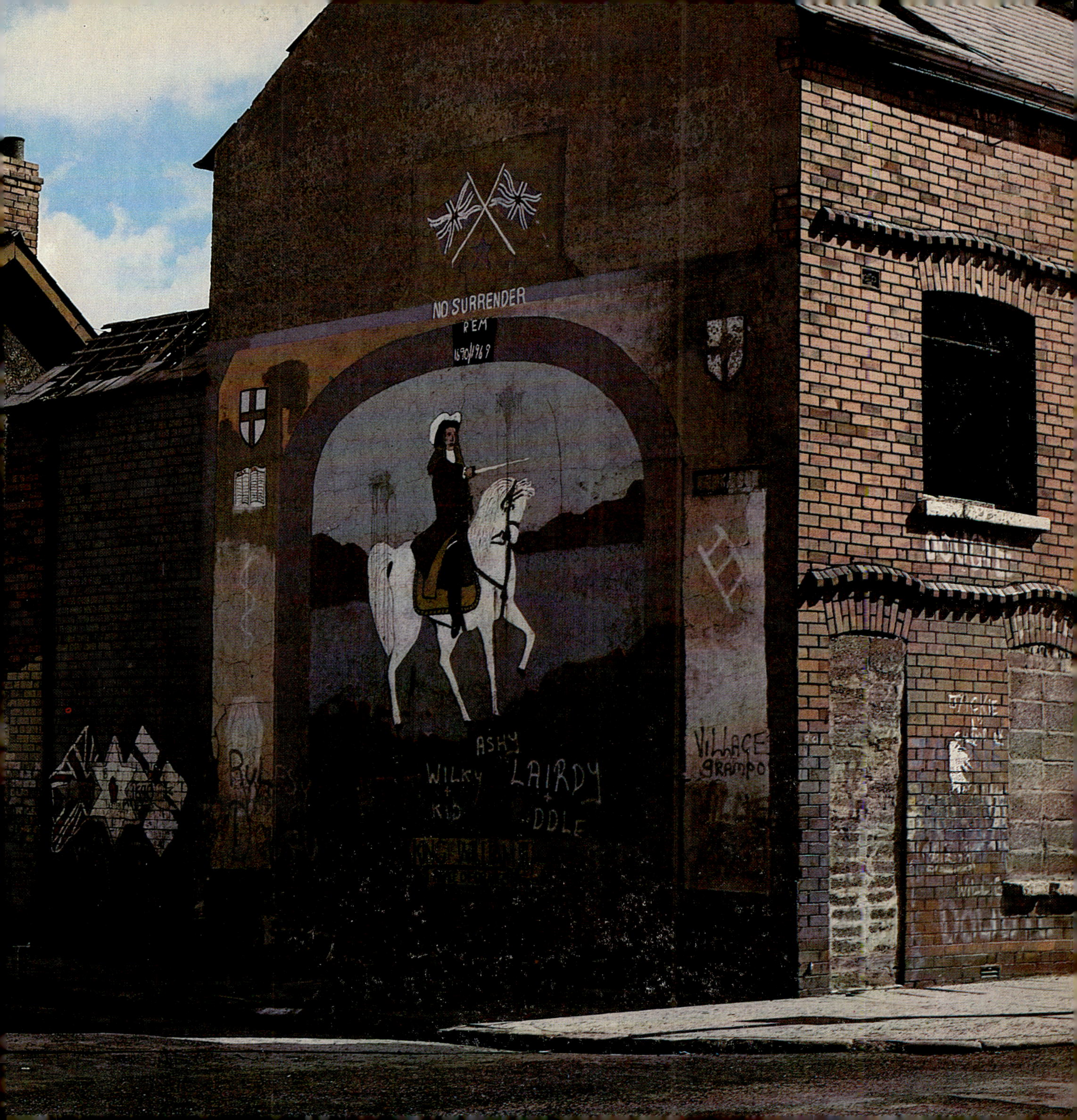
NO SURRENDER
REM
1690/1969
ASHY
WILKY
LAIRDY
KID
VILLAGE
GRAMPO

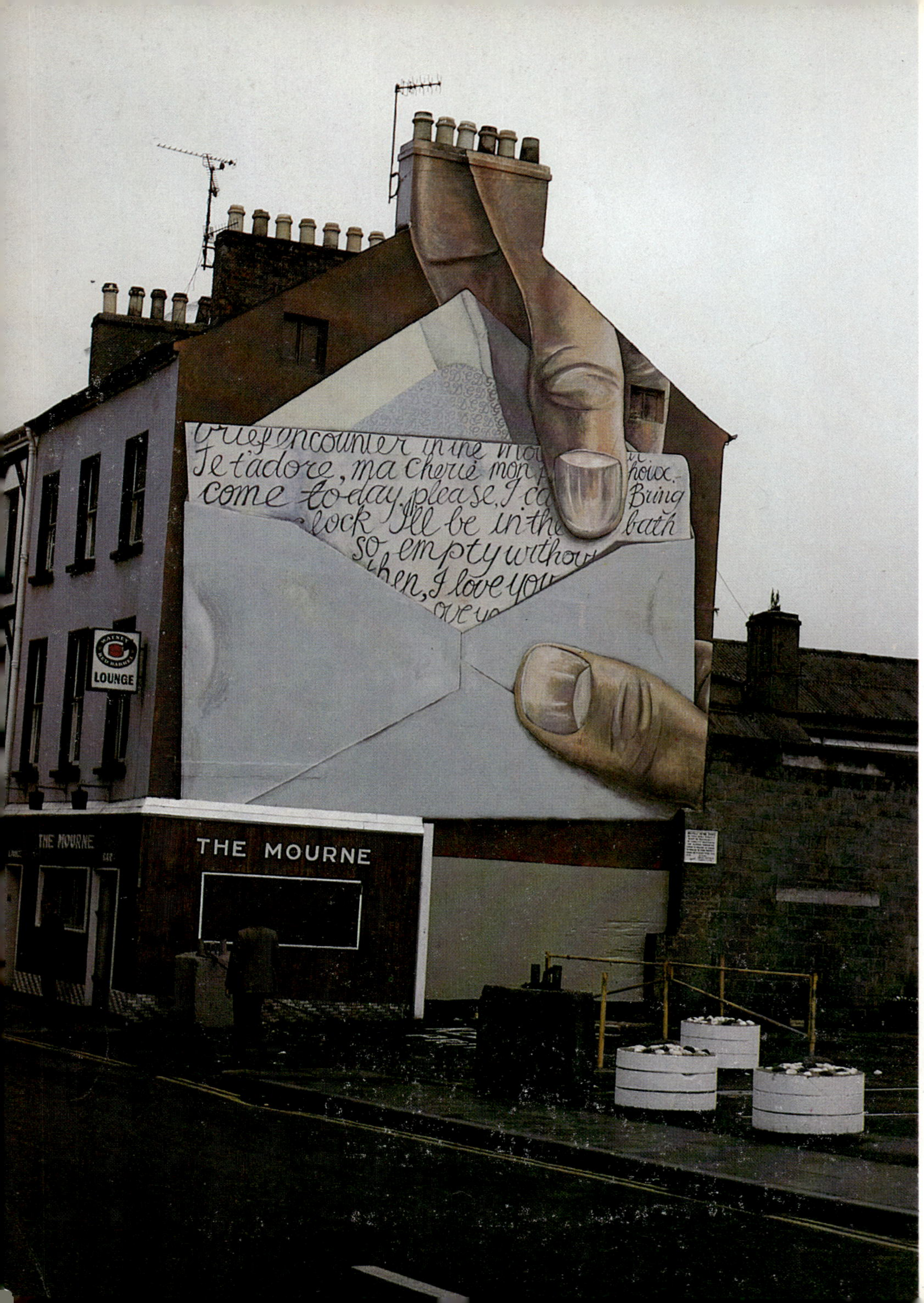

This public information-type mural, *Brief Encounter,* by Noel Millar, is on the Mourne Bar in Foyle Street, Londonderry, and seems to reflect the sad state of affairs in the city. The mural was financed by the Arts Council of Northern Ireland.

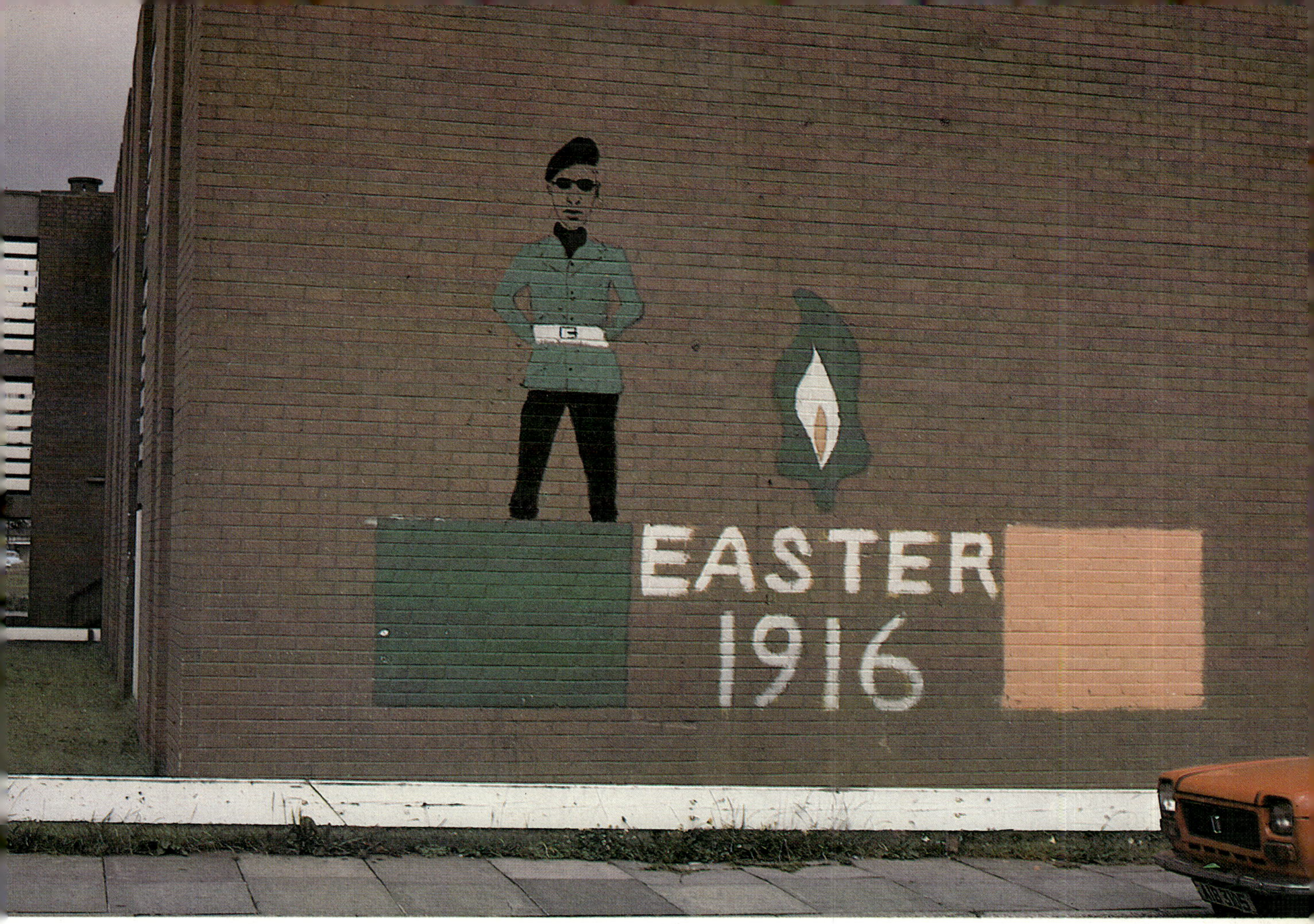

This design of the Irish tricolour and the torch signifying that the spirit of the 1916 Easter uprising is still alive, is to be found at the main entrance to the Bogside, Londonderry.

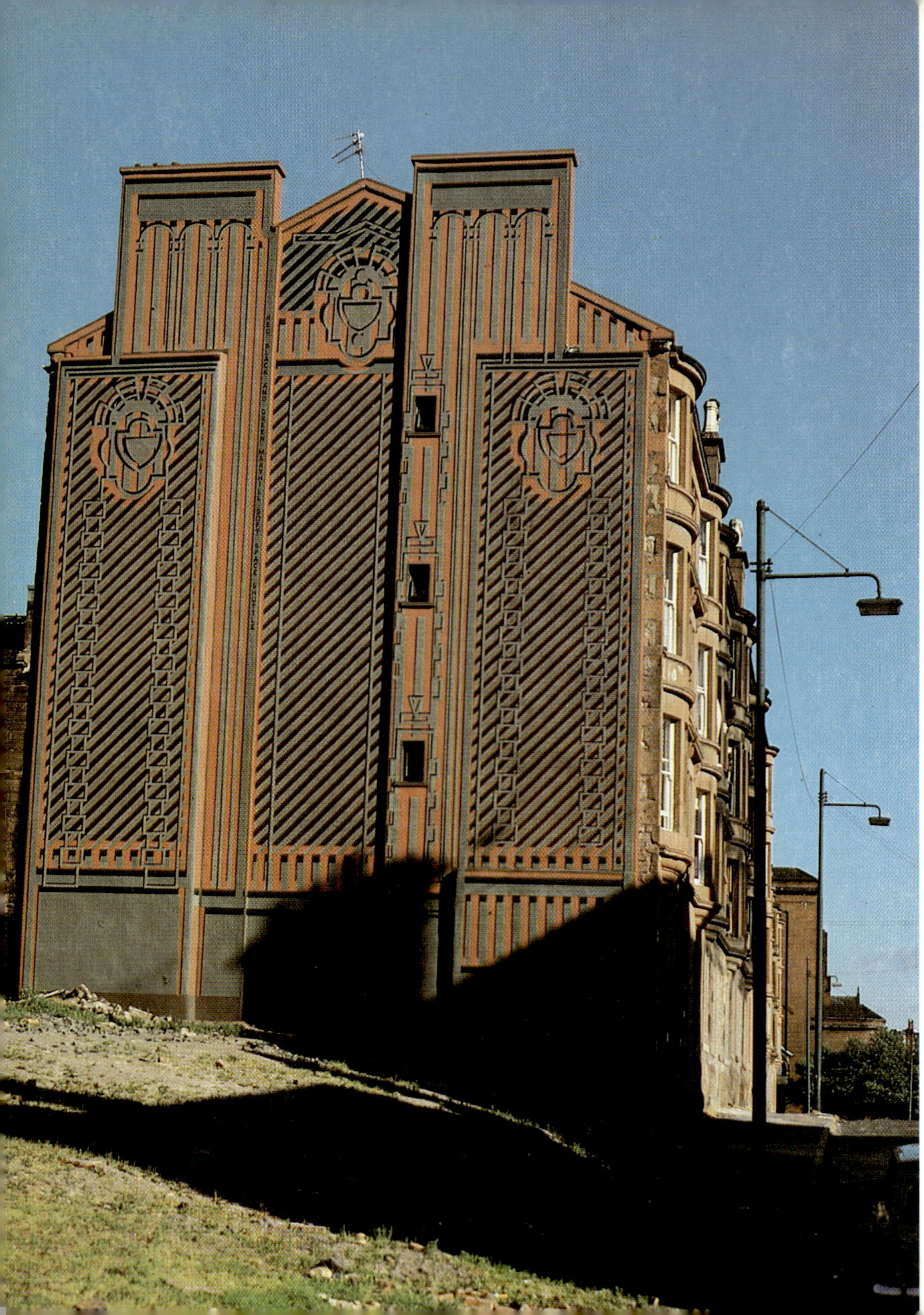

Tim Armstrong had two main objectives in painting this architectonic decoration in Ancroft Street, Glasgow. He wanted, firstly, to harmonize the colour and scale of the design with the building and its surroundings and, secondly, to provide a decoration that would be attractive to the community.

Aided by the Dundee Housing Association, Robert McGilvray painted two similar murals, *Outro* and *Intro,* in the Court Street area of the city. *Outro,* shown here, was completed in 1976. Its exotic subject contrasts with the semi-derelict urban jungle surrounding it.

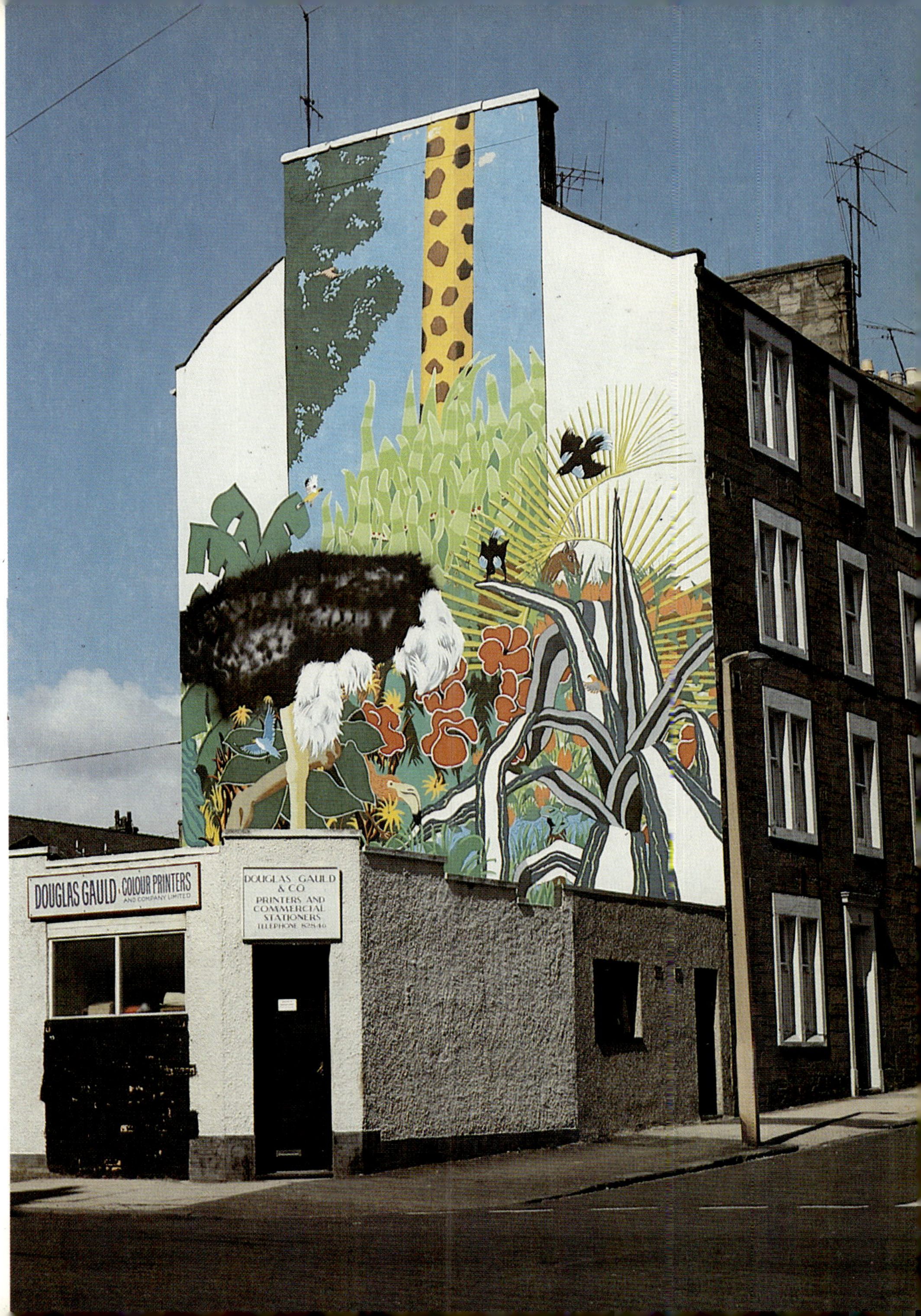

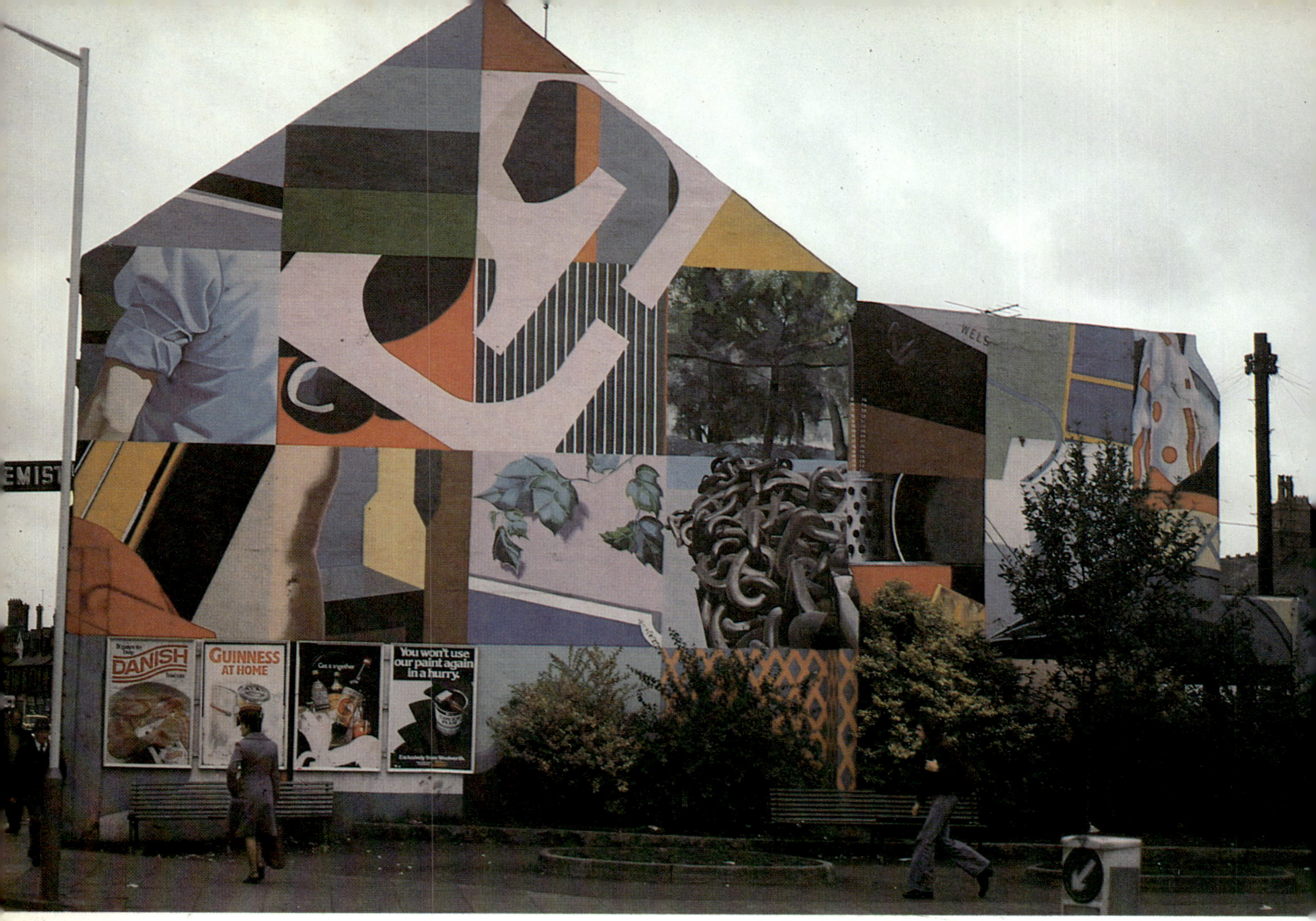

This topographical mural, organized by the Wallsend Arts Centre, was painted by Duncan Newton with the assistance of local people. The details are based on everyday scenes of the shipbuilding town of Wallsend.

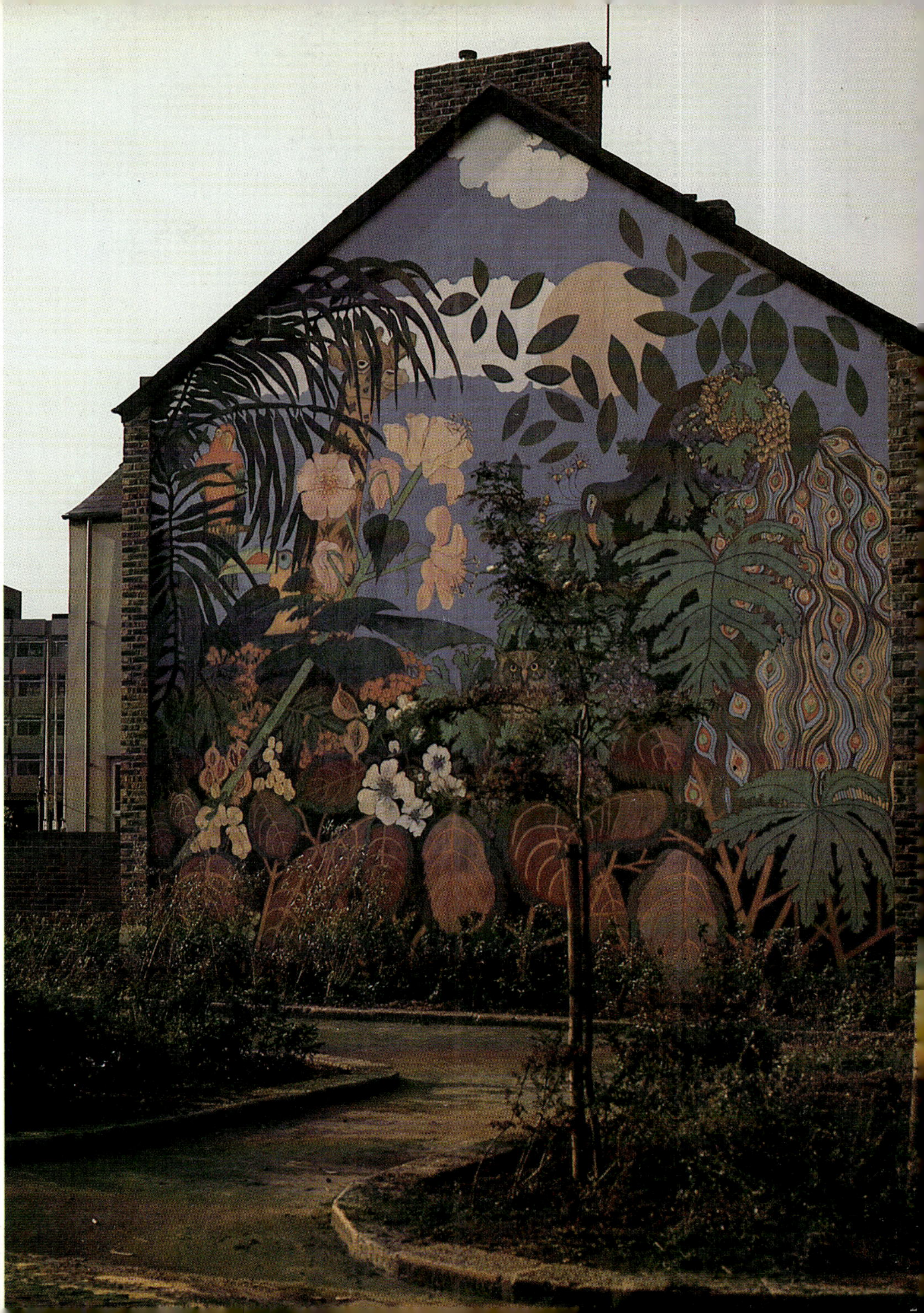

The *Bird of Paradise in the Jungle,* by Tricia Gilman, was painted in one of the housing rehabilitation areas of Jesmond, Newcastle upon Tyne. As this mural shows, a designer can adapt colours that are found in nature to an urban setting.

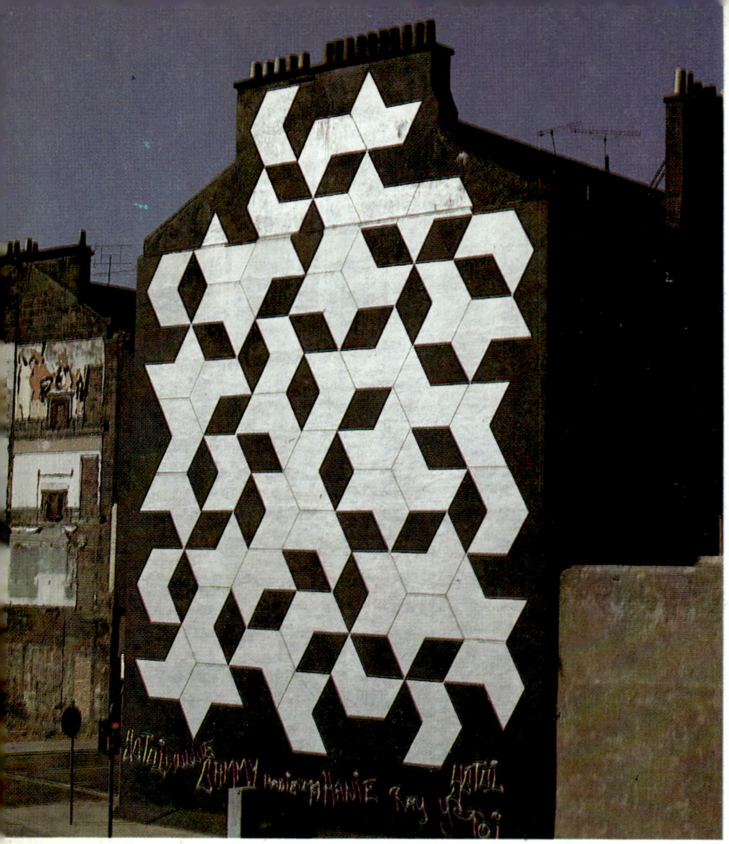

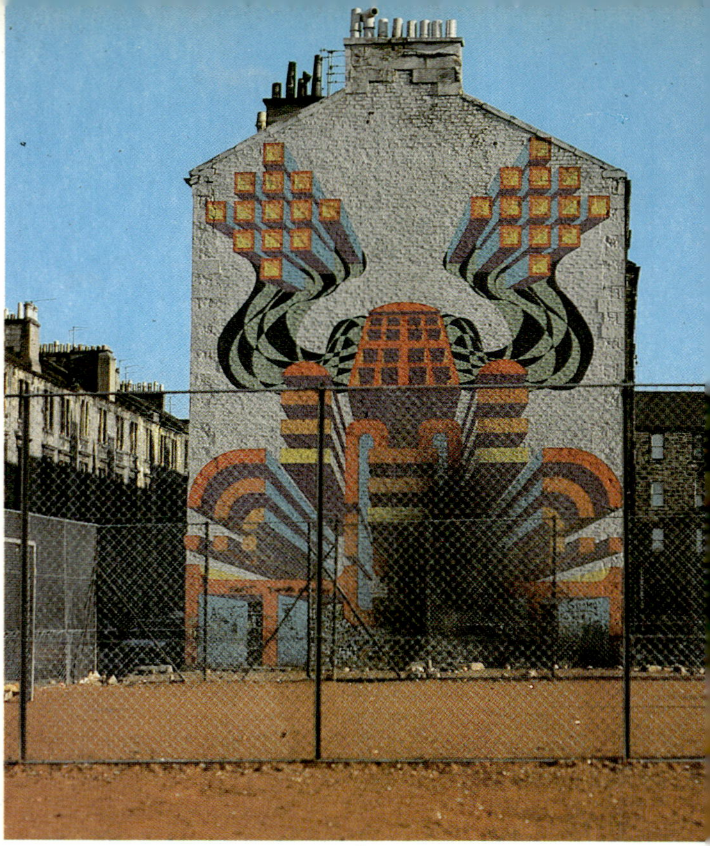

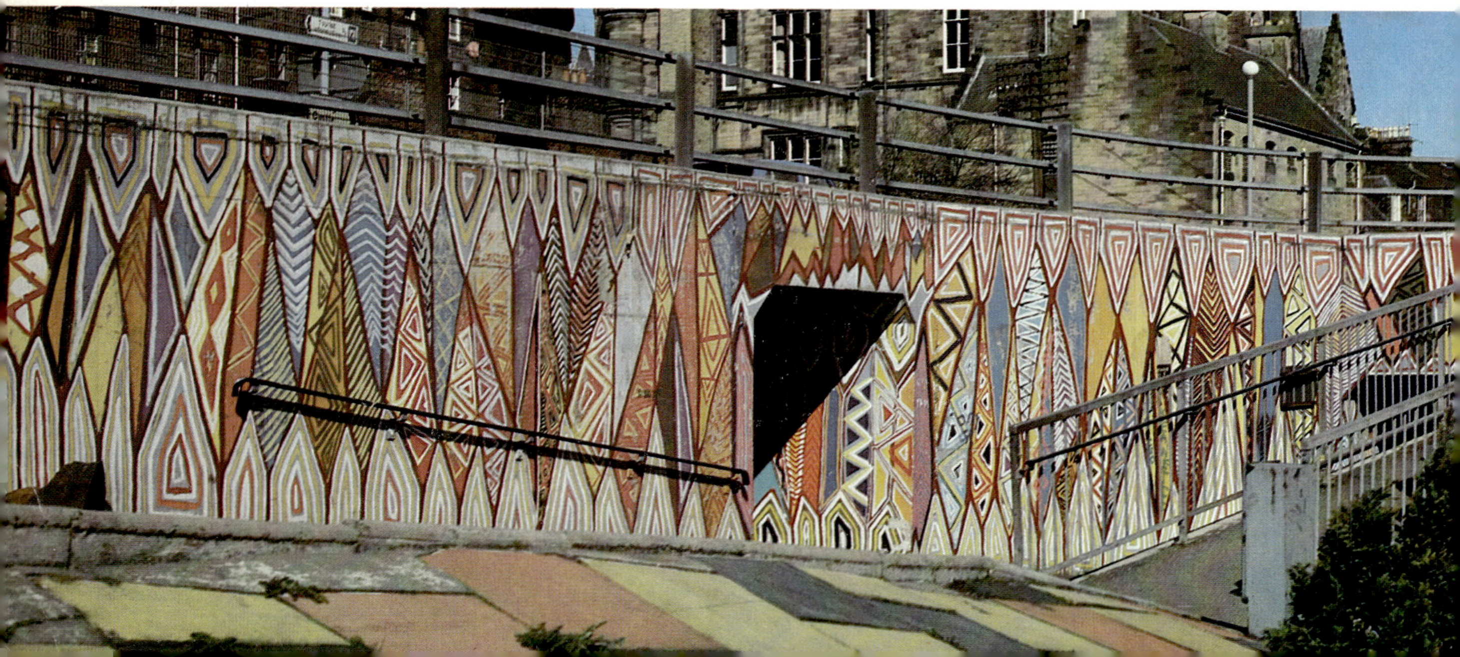

Opposite

left, above: The Scottish Arts Council funded this large-scale decoration, called *Hex*, which is located in St. Georges Road, Glasgow, and normally viewed at speed from one of the city's expressways. It is painted by Stan Bell, but signed by a local gangleader in a graffiti-like style in an attempt to claim the wall and to persuade others to scrawl elsewhere.

right, above: John McColl's *Klapa H.*, known locally as the Bionic Frog, in Bell Grove, Denniston, is, together with *Hex*, one of the early Scottish Arts Council mural schemes. The problem of graffiti has been tackled here by leaving an area free for scribbling within the lower part of the design.

below: A section of a pedestrian subway in Sterling decorated by school-children. The former stark concrete walls are decorated with designs based on the slogans and graffiti they are trying to hide.

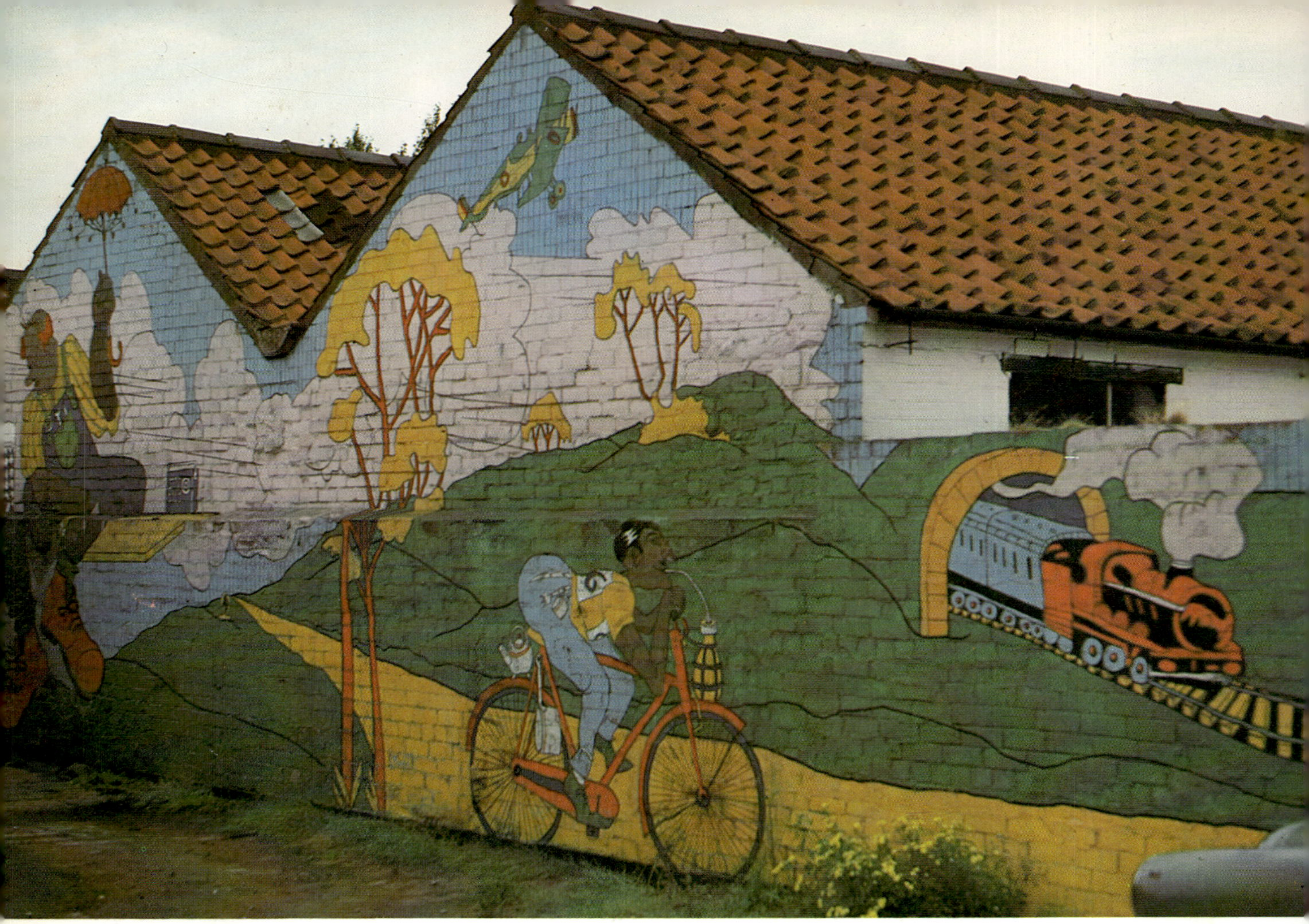

The owner of this garage in Mill Road, Lincoln, asked the scene painter, Kari Furre, to brighten up the drab wall next to his working area.

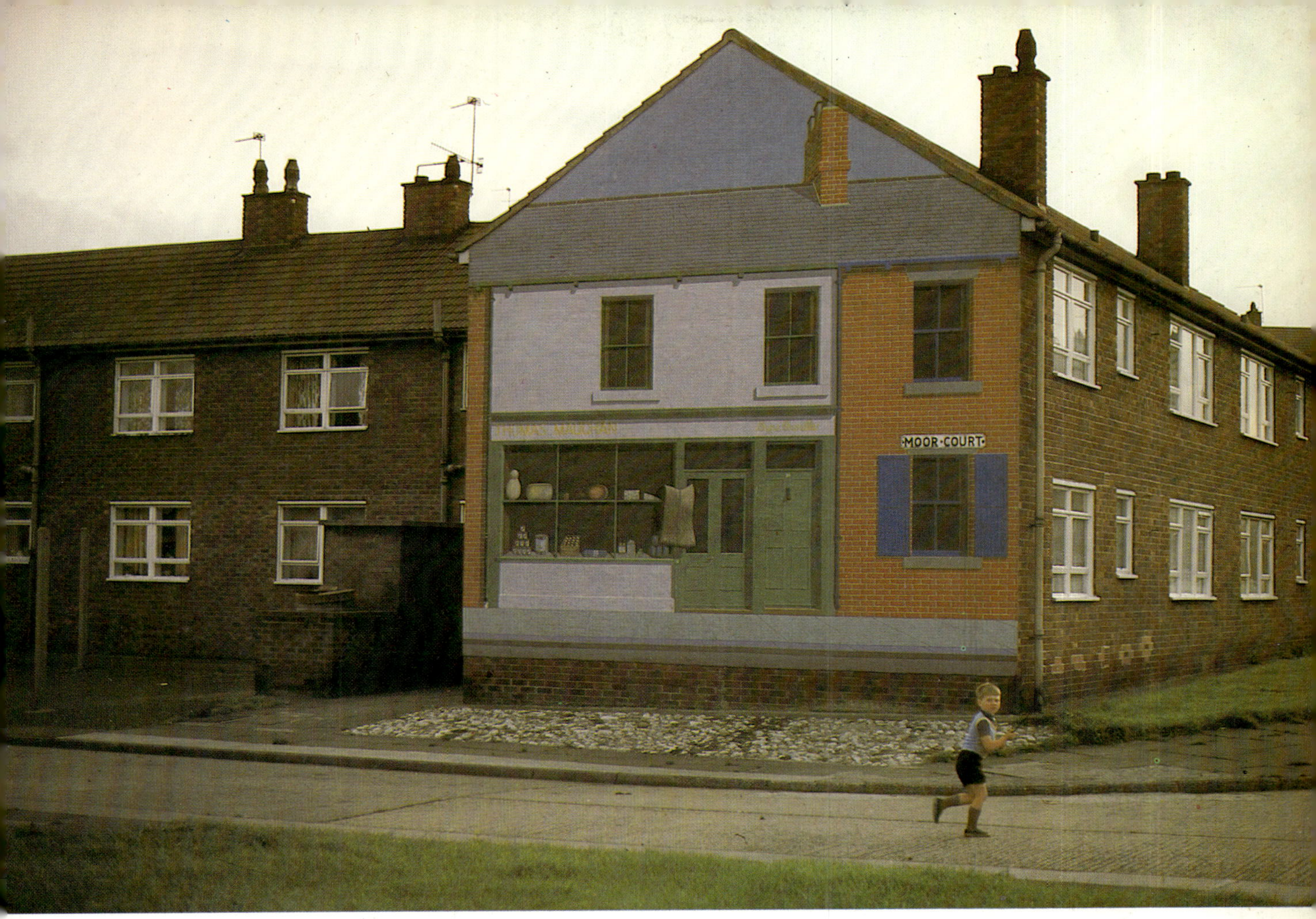

This old seamen's general store by Ken Watts, located in Moor Court, Sunderland, owes its existence to the initiative of a local community worker and to the Sunderland Arts Centre. The mural is like one of the artist's canvas paintings. Because of planning regulations it is raised above the ground to avoid rising damp.

Case study

AN ACCOUNT OF THE VAN GOGH BUS SHELTER PROJECT, BURY, GREATER MANCHESTER

INTENTION

The aim was to continue a series of wall painting experiments, this time with a group of schoolchildren at Elton Secondary Modern School in Bury, Greater Manchester. The youngsters chosen were in the final summer term of their school lives and were idly awaiting their freedom. The idea of cleaning up and adding a blaze of colour to a local wall near the school was greeted with great enthusiasm by the eight or so pupils since they had seen other wall paintings around the town. They were very eager and full of suggestions, most of which were for commercial hero worship images such as pop groups, footballers, racing drivers etc. The group consisted mainly of pupils who had a reasonable amount of confidence in their artistic ability. It contained fifty per cent of the fifth formers who regularly attended school after the final C.S.E. examinations.

CHOOSING THE SITE

The first step was to send the group out in pairs looking for painting locations. Once they found an appropriate site they were instructed to draw both it and the surrounding features. Most walls were not convenient to paint. They were either private property or hidden from view, and often had extremely rough surfaces.

Finally, we noticed that the nearby village public bus/toilet shelter had been vandalized and was in a bad state of repair. This shelter was used by the Walshaw village community and it was a meeting place for local teenagers at night, in fact it was their only amenity.

We enquired at the local transport office but discovered five days later that the borough cleansing department was responsible for the premises and for giving us permission.

WAITING FOR PERMISSION

Permission took three weeks, which in terms of public property is very quick. In the meantime the kids were becoming restless doing all sorts of designs but not knowing the exact location or whether they would have enough time left at school to complete the project. During this period they were asked to obtain paint from their relations or neighbours. Some paint was bought from a limited amount of school funds.

One morning we made a survey in order to monitor the local response to such a project. This was a good public relations exercise for the children. All the people interviewed were in favour of having the bus shelter cleaned up and painted.

Incidentally, during this time, I discovered that the Bury Town Council were planning to repair and redecorate the public toilets, which meant that our scheme would be saving them money.

DESIGN IDEAS

Initially the children drew their designs for each of the chosen sites, eventually tackling the problem of painting the bus shelter. Their ideas varied from flowers, landscapes, motor cars, large pop star portraits to seaside and boat scenes. We also looked through a selection of art books for inspiration and it soon became apparent that they all liked the work of Vincent Van Gogh.

Mainly because of the lack of time and the inhibited attempts by the children (due to the awkward shapes of the bus shelter), I decided that existing paintings should be used. It would be far easier copying from a book than using the children's drawings. Luckily Van Gogh paintings were compatible with the original designs, that is, the flowers, landscapes and large portraits. Also, Van Gogh's painting of his own room seemed very appropriate for the shelter's waiting-room. One side

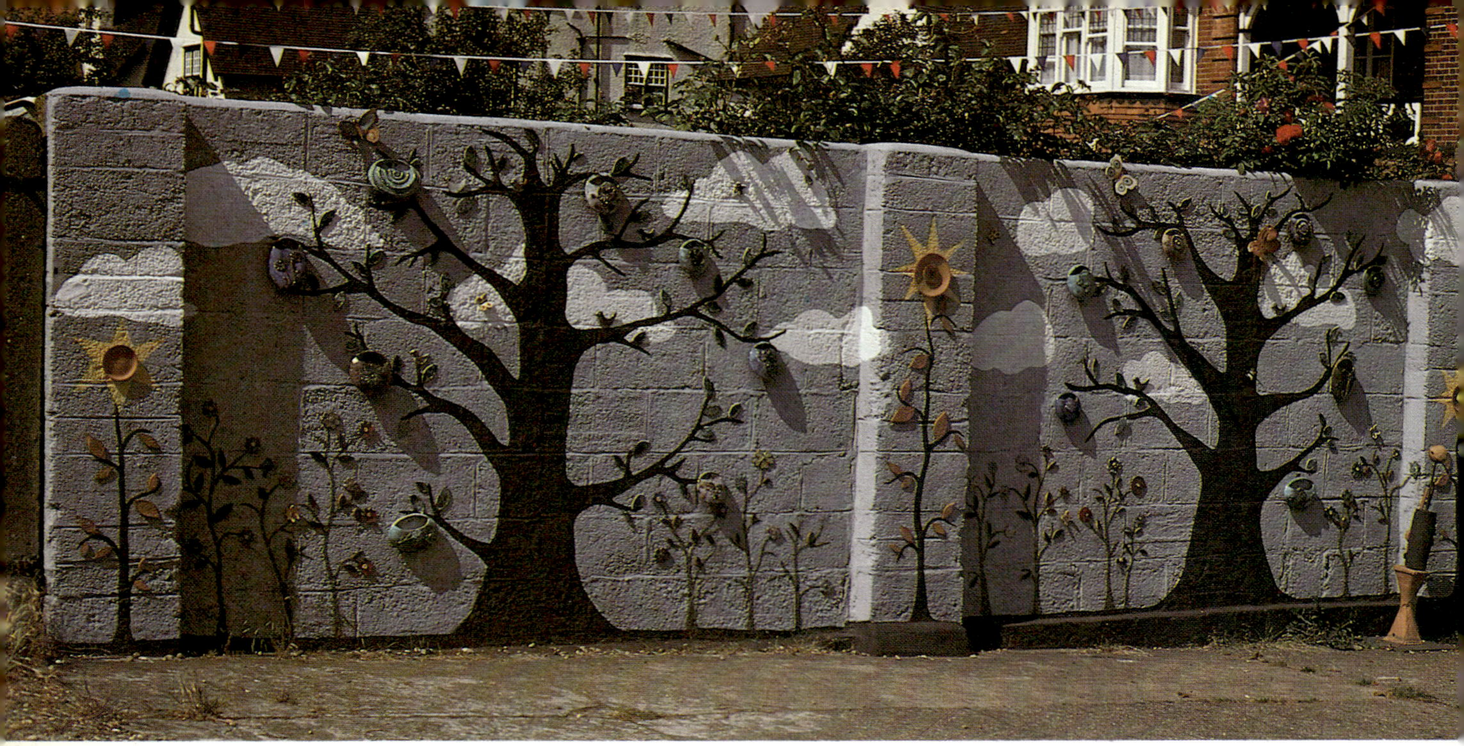

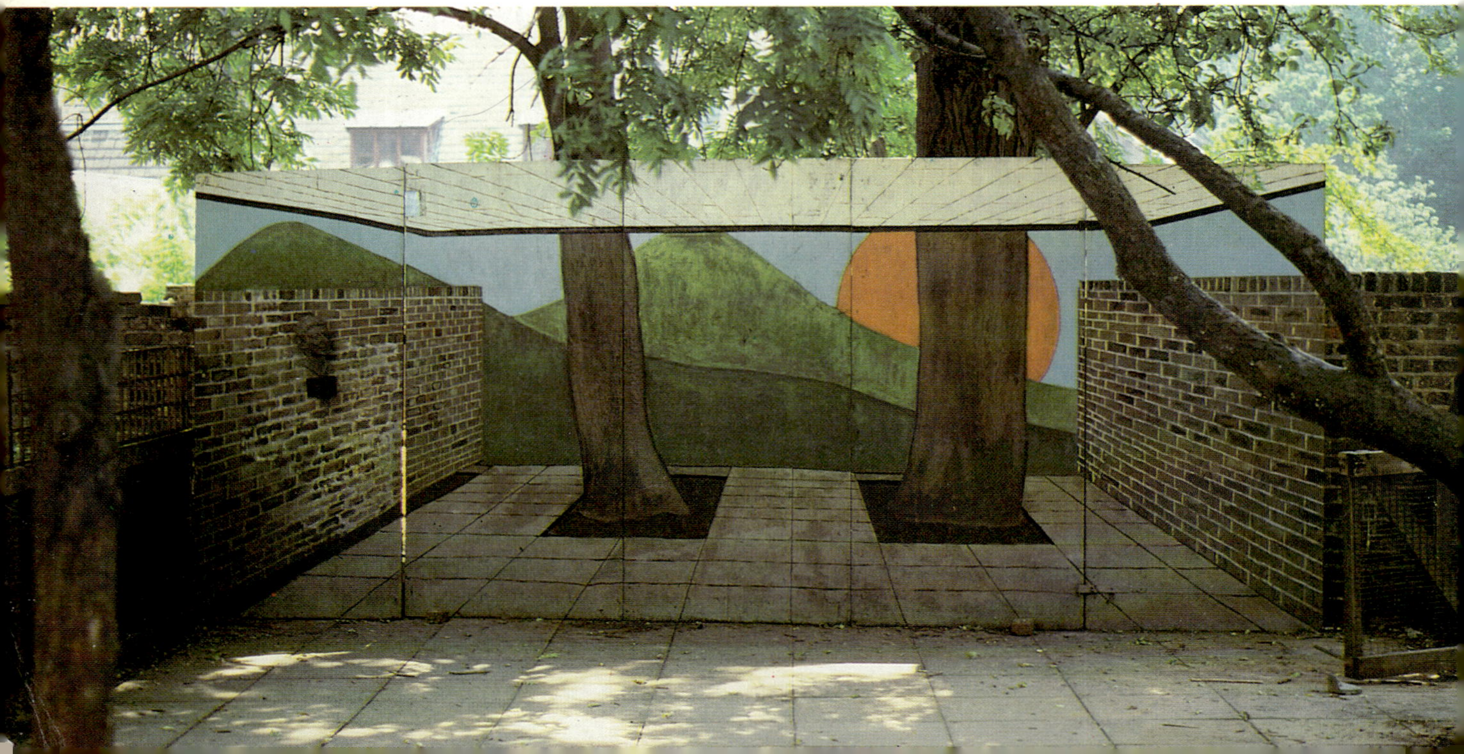

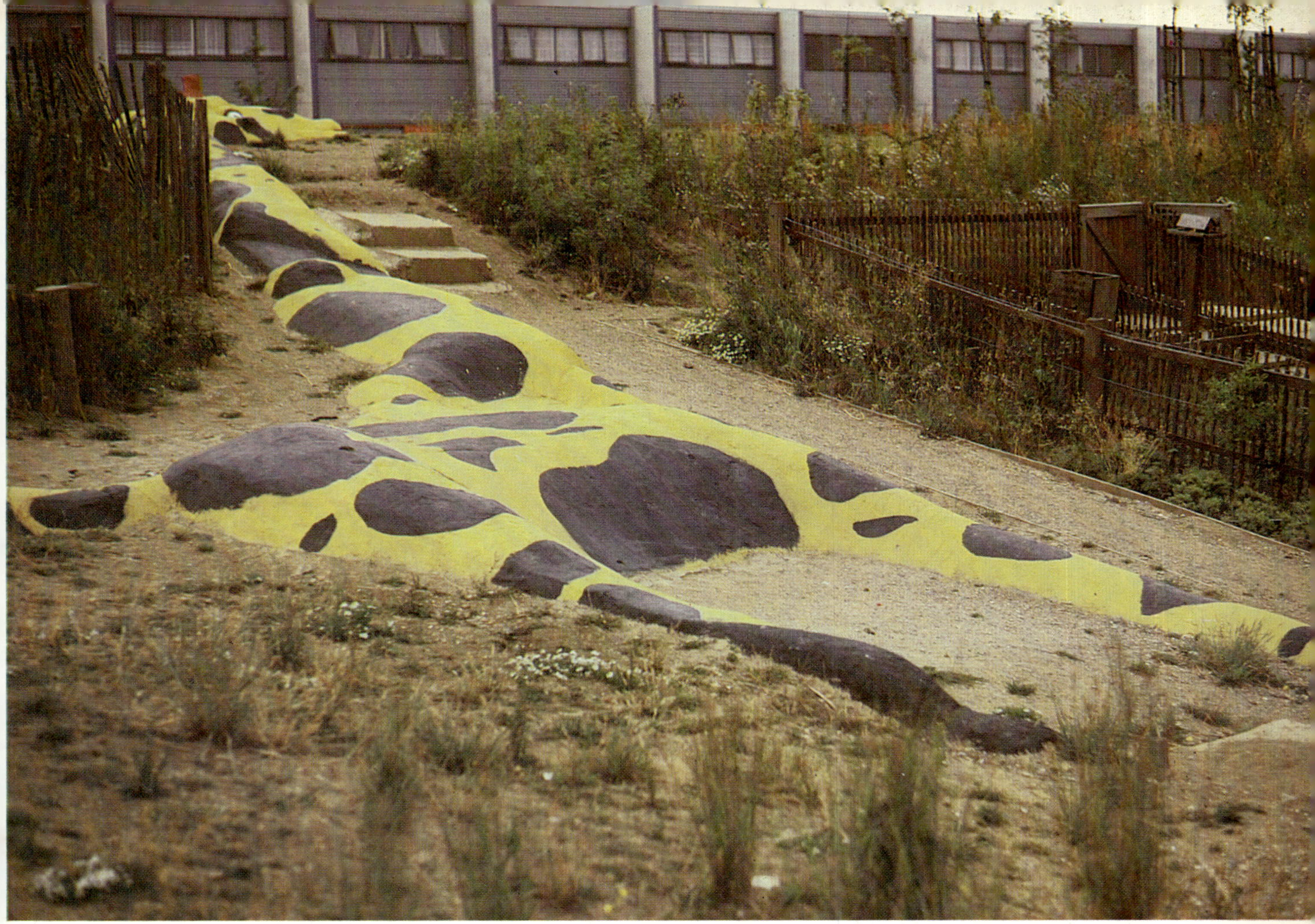

above: This unusual giraffe in Netherfield was the idea of thirteen-year-old Marion Forbes and painted under the supervision of Liz Leyh, the community artist in residence at Milton Keynes. The giraffe measures thirty feet in length.

left, above: Painted in 1973 by Adrian Farncombe, this creation covers what he called a despicable concrete wall in the courtyard of his pottery business.

left, below: Peter Rich's mural on a wooden fence in his back garden in Dunboyne Road, London, creates the illusion of space. The artist was probably aware of the ancient Roman tradition of painting an illusionary landscape within a courtyard.

of the design was now going to be 'Starry, starry night' from the pop song they all knew and the other, a large portrait of Van Gogh with his bandaged ear, a story which caught the imagination of the kids. On the front of the shelter, the earlier flower designers were asked to paint sunflowers and irises.

These designs were mainly dictated by me but they were not preconceived images. They came from ideas which stemmed from discussions with the pupils and were received with reasonable enthusiasm.

SECTIONAL RESPONSIBILITIES

There was as near as possible a freedom of choice with each person usually choosing the section which corresponded to his original suggestion. This ruling was not strictly adhered to as paint shortages delayed certain sections. Eventually, however, each person managed to complete his task. One lad was amazed at the massive face he had constructed, a feat he had previously imagined to be beyond him.

There was some dispute among the pupils towards individuals. 'I don't want to work with him. He'll only mess about', was the kind of comment which later proved to be unfounded.

INITIAL PREPARATIONS

After three weeks of waiting, ten eager children began to scrub and brush the walls both inside and out of the toilets and waiting-room. The mortar was covered with primers which supposedly contained lime restrictive qualities.

As this was completed we painted the undercoats, first on the ceilings and inside surfaces. Emulsion paints were used on the brickwork, and gloss paints were used on the woodwork.

DRAWING AND MARKING OUT

The pupils traced out the images from the paintings by Van Gogh and then added a grid system, using this technique to transfer the images onto the walls. There were perspective and proportion problems with the room picture which required my assistance.

In the 'Starry, starry night', pictures of known places were introduced such as the local parish church and a landscape which included surrounding hills and two towers built in the district. For the sake of simplicity each drawing consisted of an absolute minimum of basic components. Whenever there was any difficulty in producing the correct shape, I instructed the pupils to familiarize themselves with the objects by first drawing them onto paper. Some difficulty was experienced in joining the individual sections.

PAINTING

Eventually we acquired all the paints, with one last school week in which to complete the project. With much overtime, the flowers and 'Starry, starry night' sections were completed.

Unfortunately, the room presented a vast problem and by the time the children had left school it was still unfinished.

The Van Gogh portrait was also finished off during the school holidays, by a very keen pupil and myself. Other sections also received attention.

The kids were usually too impatient and easily satisfied, believing their section to be complete before it actually was. However, they responded very favourably to this criticism. We found that gloss paints were not suitable for brick surfaces as they were too easily scratched. Other minor problems were not always having enough brushes or step-ladders, and also paint dripping onto the pavement and onto the kids' overalls.

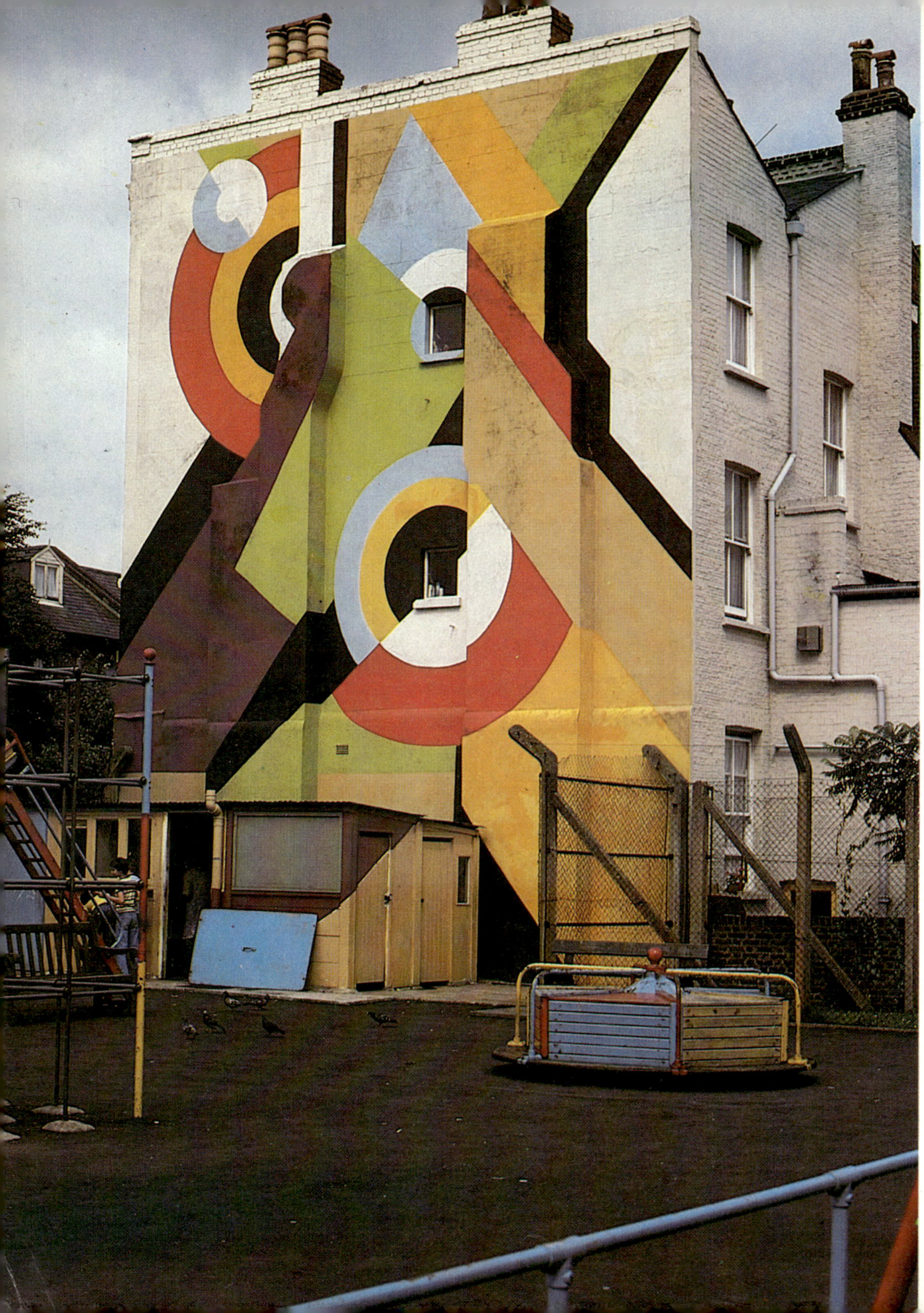

This bold abstract design in Iverson Road, London, was done by architecture students in order to break up the surface of the wall visually and to disguise the attendant's hut.

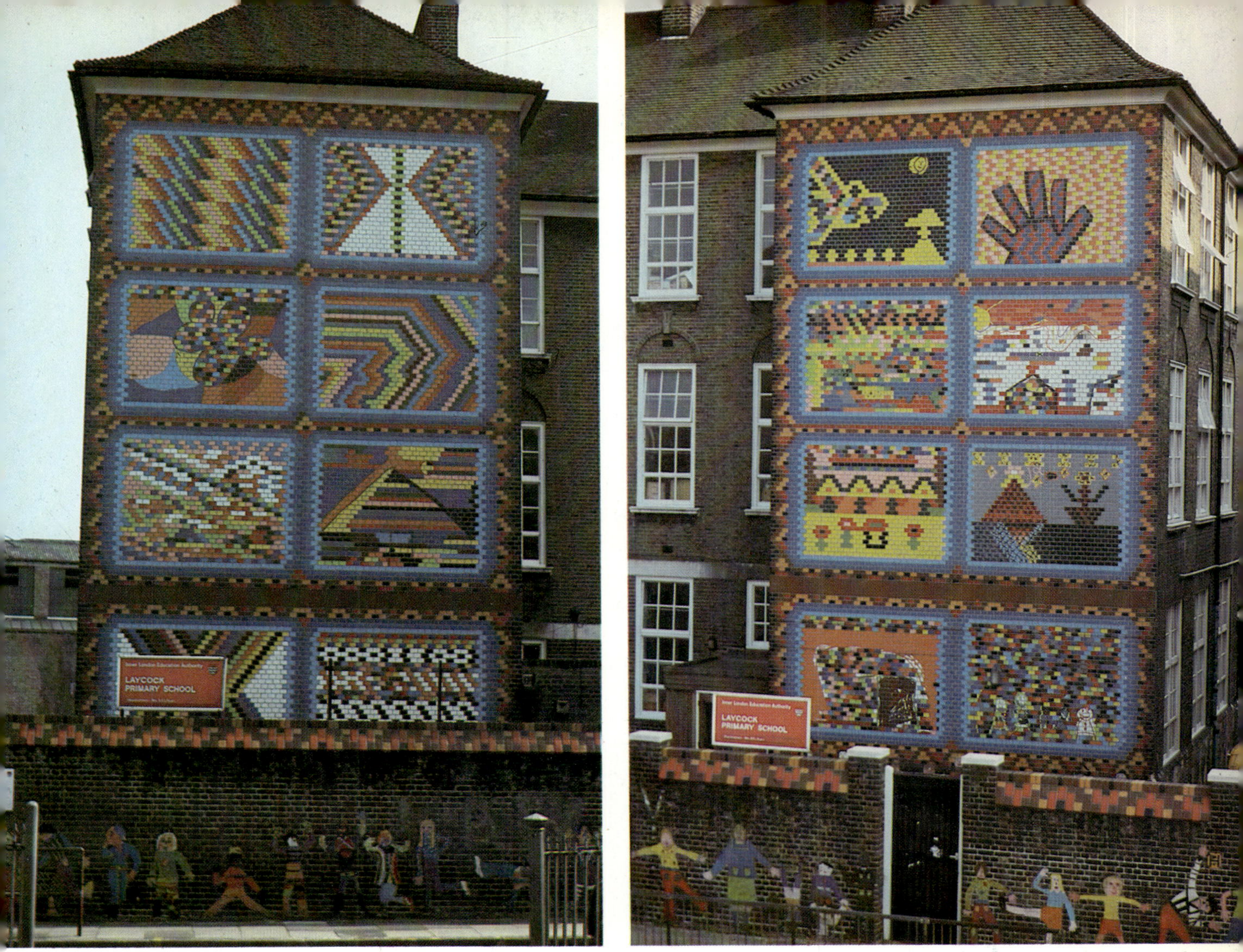

Part of the decorations by David Cashman and Roger Fagin on the Laycock School, Islington. It was decided that the two gable fronts of the building should show the kind of activity that went on within the school. Each of the three hundred and twenty pupils were presented with silk-screen prints of brickwork on to which they were asked to paint designs. The final sixteen designs were chosen after discussion with the children, teachers, and parents. The border designs, painted by the artists, are a special feature of these murals.

CHILDREN'S PARTICIPATION

This scheme brought out the vast creative spirit that is within each child provided that it is suitably channelled and given the chance to express itself. The children were working on Sundays and even in the evenings, which is very rare for any school project. There was an obvious pleasure in being out of the school and in the community, acting the role of real working people.

Unfortunately, once the school had broken up, they either started a job or were on holidays. This however, gave the local kids a chance to help. Two or three assisted, which was very gratifying as it was these teenagers who would use the shelter at night.

On the final day of term, the most delinquent pupil in the school offered his services. This under-achieving boy had found an interest which the school's ordinary curriculum had failed to arouse.

COMMUNITY RESPONSE

The shelter became a local talking point, the older people conversing with the youths and encouraging them to continue their work.

A local newspaper made it a front page story, and there were letters in the paper congratulating the pupils on their decorum and claiming that this was a way of beating vandalism.

People offered the walls of their houses to be painted. A couple of adult passers-by even helped with the painting for an afternoon, and neighbours regularly brought bottles of pop, tea, and sweets.

CONCLUSIONS

This project was a success in many ways but mainly because of the community response. Everybody wanted the shelter to be cleaned up.

Overleaf

left: Desmond Rochfort and Dave Binnington, working under the name of the Public Art Workshop, were given large grants to produce these two murals at Royal Oak, London. The artists aimed at creating a public art that would be critical and visually demanding. The theme of work was chosen and considered appropriate to a site that, to a great extent, is viewed by people either going to or from their place of employment. The murals are painted with silicon-based mineral paints and are expected to last as long as the surface of the motorway structure.

right, above: This is one of a series of murals painted by Emily Young in order to humanize a stretch of the Westway motorway between Ladbroke Grove and Portobello Road, London.

right, below: This mural of skateboarders can be seen from the motorway leading to Shepherd's Bush, London. It was painted by members of the Harrow Club and supervised by Dave Bent, the craftsman in residence.

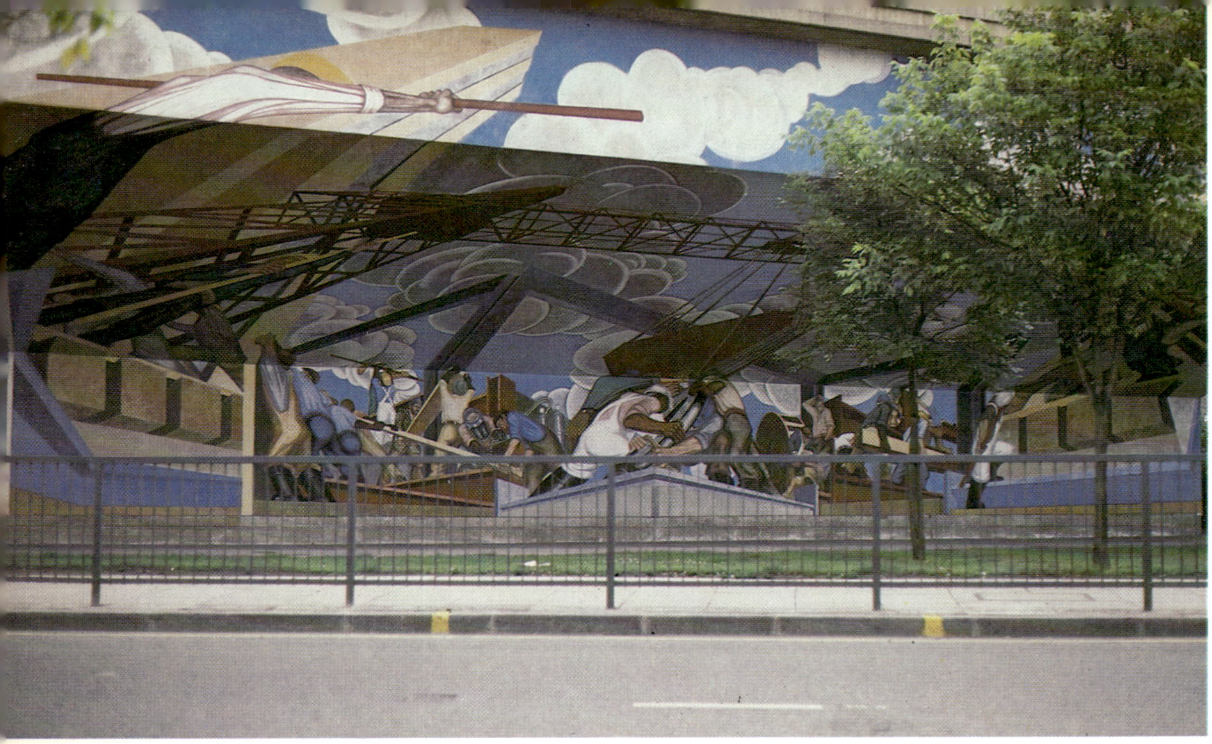

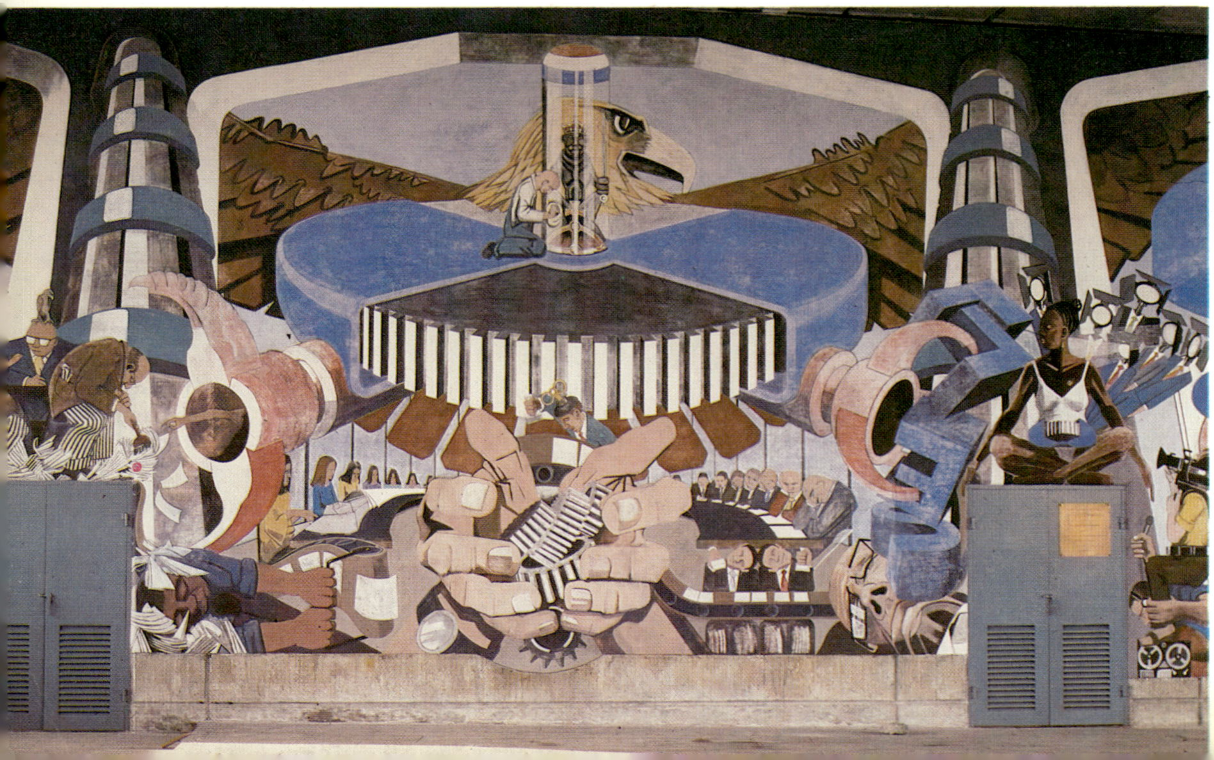

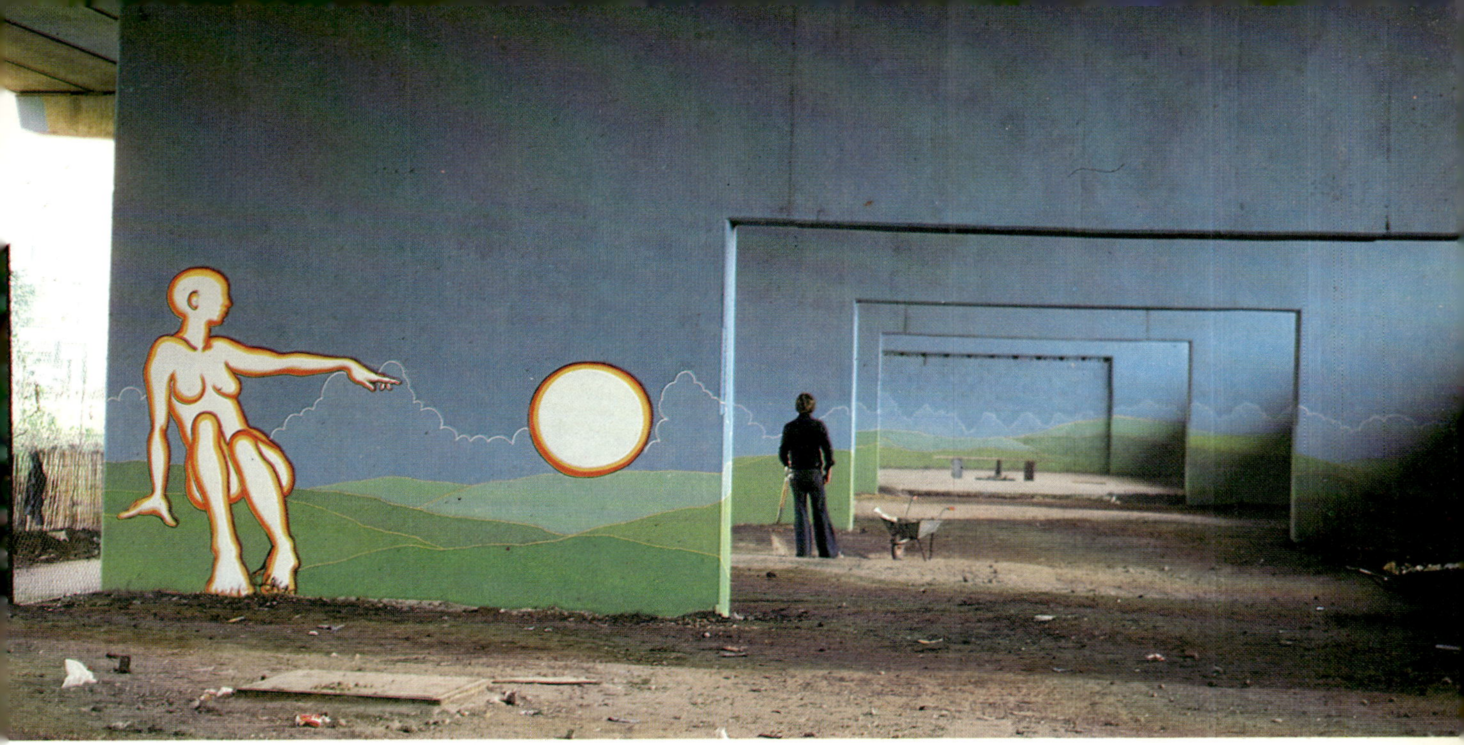

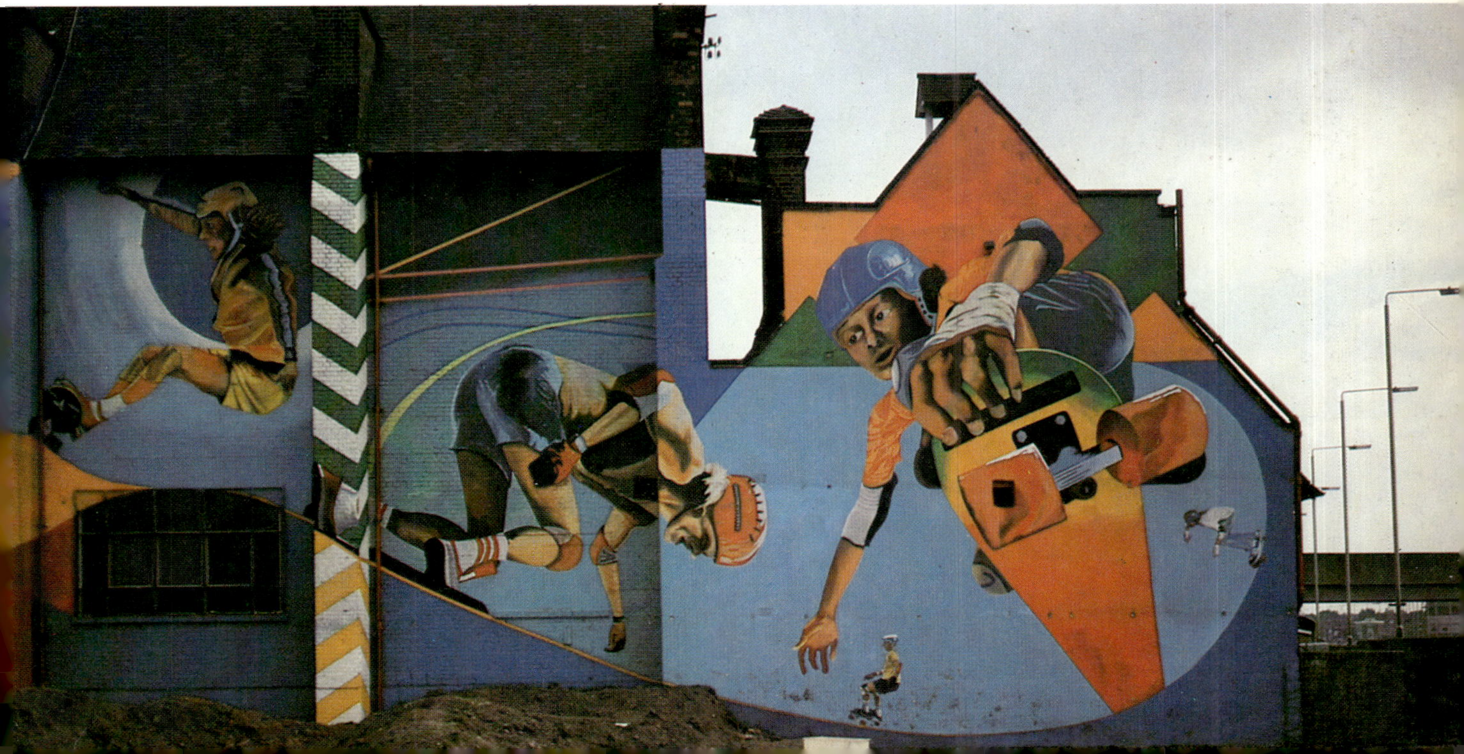

In the end this was achieved. One could again sit inside the waiting-room or use the toilets.

The coming together of elderly folk and young adolescents was another rare feature of this activity. The pupils deserved every credit for their patience and hard work. Educationally the scheme was very valuable, not only for the attainment of certain decorating skills but as a lesson in art appreciation.

Ideally, there should have been more participation from the local youths who, although they did help occasionally, suffered from a lack of interest and concentration. This could have stemmed from the fact that the project was connected with school. A continual annoyance was the negative attitude adopted by some people: 'How long do you think the mural will last before it is destroyed?' This question does touch upon a major problem, but if everyone had such an attitude nothing would ever be created.

The shelter will always cause comment and interest, especially by strangers. On the other hand it is hoped that the local residents are not eventually nauseated by the bright colours. Whatever happens, this Van Gogh bus shelter is the only one of its kind in the world.

Overleaf

above: *Man and Dog Visiting Mars,* painted by Anne-Margret Bellavoine on the playground wall of the Robert Montefiore Infant School, London, was part of the 1976 Tower Hamlets Arts Project. The children produced the designs and painted the sections within their reach. The artist then tidied up their work and completed the upper section of the wall.

below: A series of jokes painted by children in London's East End. Street murals, unlike contemporary gallery paintings, often contain humour.

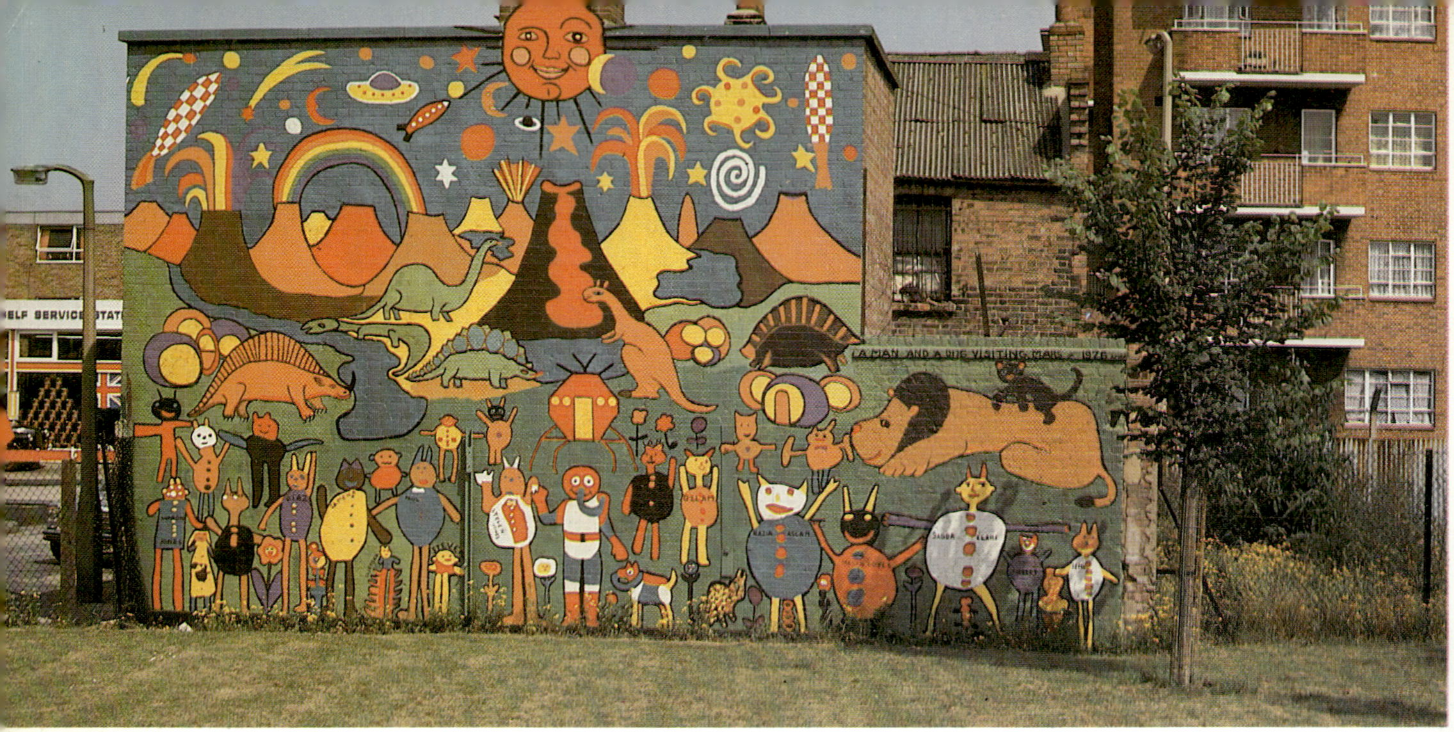

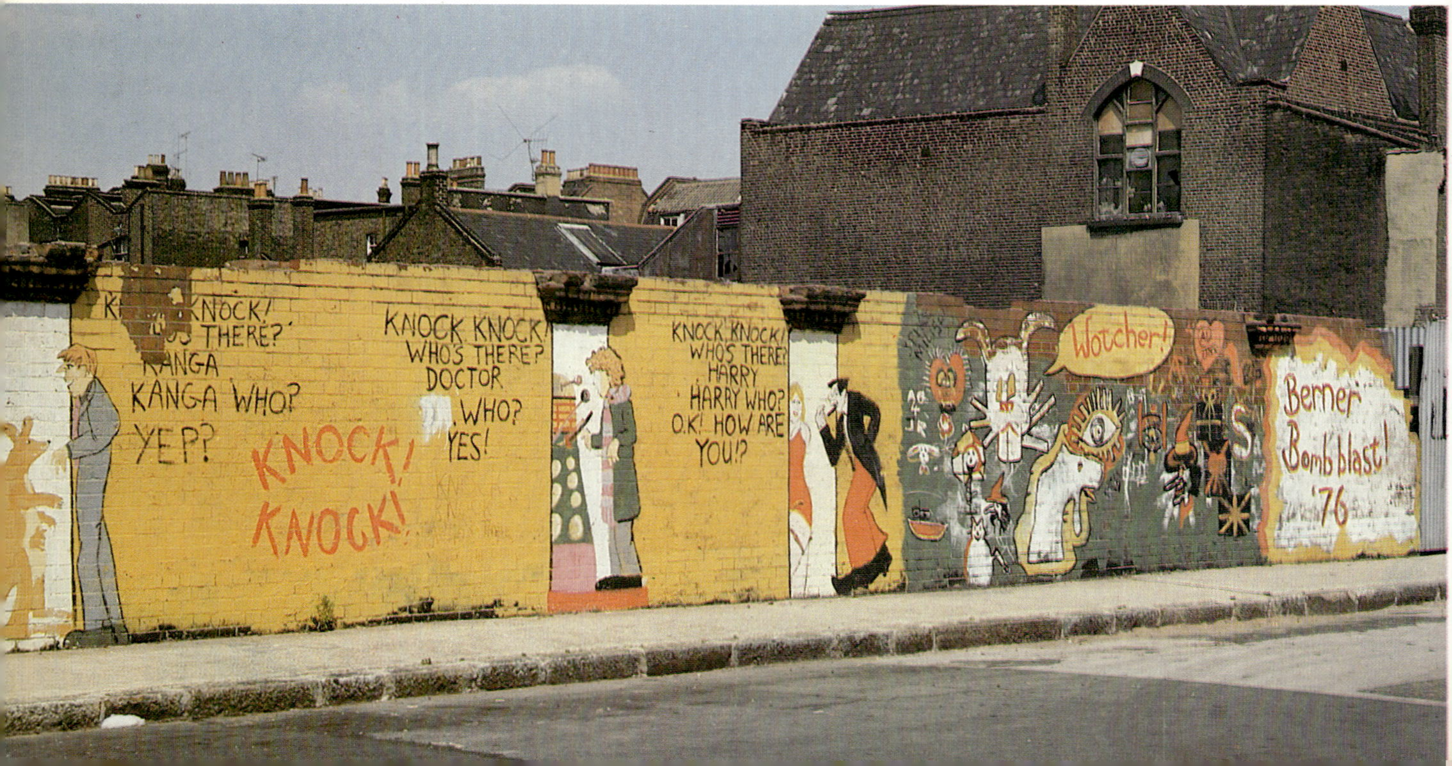
KANGA
KANGA WHO?
YEP?
KNOCK! KNOCK!
KNOCK KNOCK!
WHO'S THERE?
DOCTOR
WHO?
YES!
KNOCK KNOCK!
WHO'S THERE?
HARRY
HARRY WHO?
O.K! HOW ARE YOU!?
Wotcher!
Berner
Bomb blast!
'76

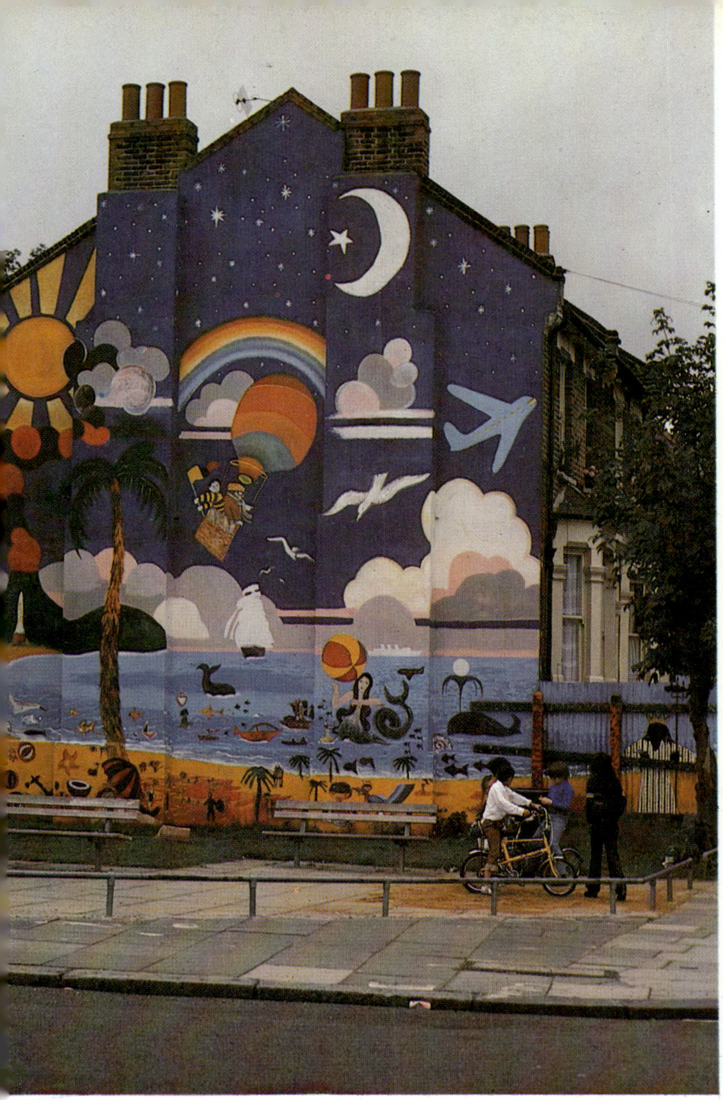

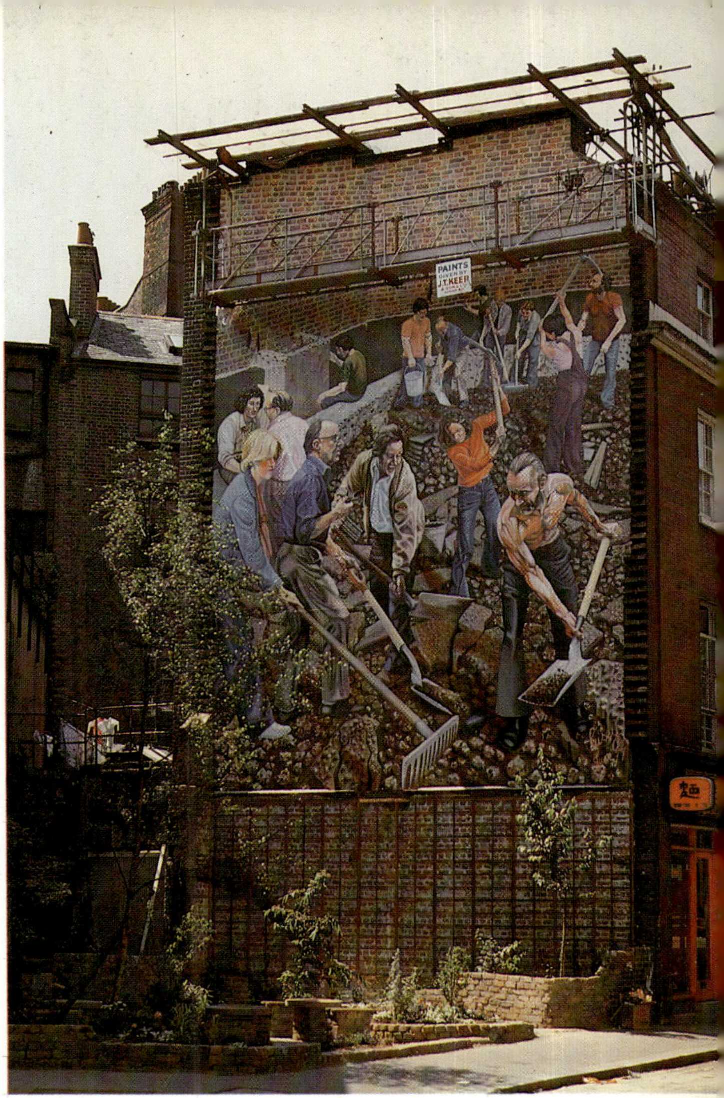

left: The Fine Heart Squad, led by Peter Carey and Phil Hartigan, painted this mural in Thornfield Road, London, with the participation of local children. Their name is an implicit criticism of the Fine Art Squad, an exclusive professional group in California.

right: Stephen Pusey painted this mural in Earlham Street, Covent Garden, London, by using slides projected onto the wall at night. The mural commemorates the local residents' success in creating the garden beneath.

Location of murals

Ashton-under-Lyne, Burlington Street
H-Bomb explosion by students from Tameside College

Ashton-under-Lyne, Market Place
Alice in Wonderland by David Vaughan

Bangor, 43 Holyhead Road
Enlarged groceries on shopfront by Ed. Povey

Barry, St. Athan
Activities at the Boys Club by Chris Halabula

Belfast, Dee Street
Antrim coast-scape by Chris Edwards and children from the area

Belfast, Donegal Road
King Billy

Belfast, South Howard Street
Jubilee flag design for Loyalist prisoners

Birmingham, Smallheath, Talfourd Street
Geometrical designs by Bryan Blumer

Bolton, Waterloo Street
Recycling waste

Bradford, behind the University
Battle of Wounded Knee by David Vaughan

Brierly Hill, Dudley Road
Welin Davit shipping mural by John Upton

Brighton, North Road, Presbyterian Church
Utopia and Hell by John Upton

Brighton, St. Mary's Middle School
Decorations based on school subjects by Nigel Austin

Burnley, Fullidge Community Centre
Portraits of club members by Walter Kershaw

Bury, Bolton Road and Ainsworth Road Bridge
Canal bridge decorations by Walter Kershaw, Eric Kean, Graham Cooper, Paul O'Reilly and others

Bury, The Precinct
Staircase Illusion by Graham Cooper

Bury, Peelway
King George V locomotive by Walter Kershaw, Eric Kean, Graham Cooper and others

Bury, Peelway
Spitfire, dog fight by Walter Kershaw, Eric Kean, Graham Cooper and others

Bury, Walshaw
Van Gogh bus shelter by Graham Cooper and schoolchildren

Cambridge, Grafton Street
Landscape, Clouds and Kite by Alan Melum-Boyce

Cardiff, Whitchurch, 67 Manor Way
Mountain Landscape by Mrs Naldrett

Conwy, Mount Pleasant Road
A mad medieval street fair by Ed. Povey

Dundee, Court Street
Intro, bird in the jungle by Robert McGilvray

Dundee, Court Street
Outro, giraffe in the jungle by Robert McGilvray

Edinburgh, Broughton Street
Wild life scenes by Michael Vivanco

Edinburgh, Craigmillar
Painted bus shelter and underpass

Edinburgh, Pilton Estate
Concrete dragon and unfinished murals by Ken Wolverton

Glasgow, Ancroft Street
Architectonic design by Tim Armstrong

Glasgow, 244 St. Georges Road
Hex by Stan Bell

Glasgow, Bellgrove, Denniston
Klapa H (known locally as the Bionic Frog) by John McColl

Glenrothes, New Town
Numerous mural decorations and painted underpasses encouraged by David Harding

Hastings, Guestlings, Friar Hill
View from the garden wall by J. D. Heys

Lincoln, Mill Road
Clown and cartoon-like landscape by Kari Furre

Livingston, New Town
Painted underpasses and render designs organized by Dennis Barnes

London, Battersea, Lavender Hill, Battersea Town Hall
Children playing by Amanda Webb and children

London, Battersea Bridge
Morgans wall, life in Wandsworth by Brian Barnes and the Wandsworth Mural Workshop

London, Belsize Park, Dunboyne Street
Trees and landscape by Peter Rich

London Bow off Mile End Road
Life in multiracial East End by Ray Walker

London, Camberwell, North Peckham Estate
Numerous murals and decorations by textile students from the Camberwell College of Art

London, Cambridge Circus, Earlham Street
Local community building a garden by Stephen Pusey

London, Camden, Chalk Farm
Paradise Bridge decoration by the Fine Heart Squad

London, Camden, Compendium Bookshop
Landscape above shop

London, Camden, Iverson Road
Bold abstract by students in architecture

London, Charlton, Floyd Road
Local community halting demolition by the Greenwich Mural Workshop

London, Covent Garden, St. Joseph's School
Playground decorations and game designs by Dave Cashman and Roger Fagin

London, Covent Garden
Painted hoardings by schoolchildren

London, Deptford, New Cross Road
Life in Deptford by students from Goldsmiths' College

London, East Ham, Wakefield Street
Quicks newsagents advertisement by Dulake

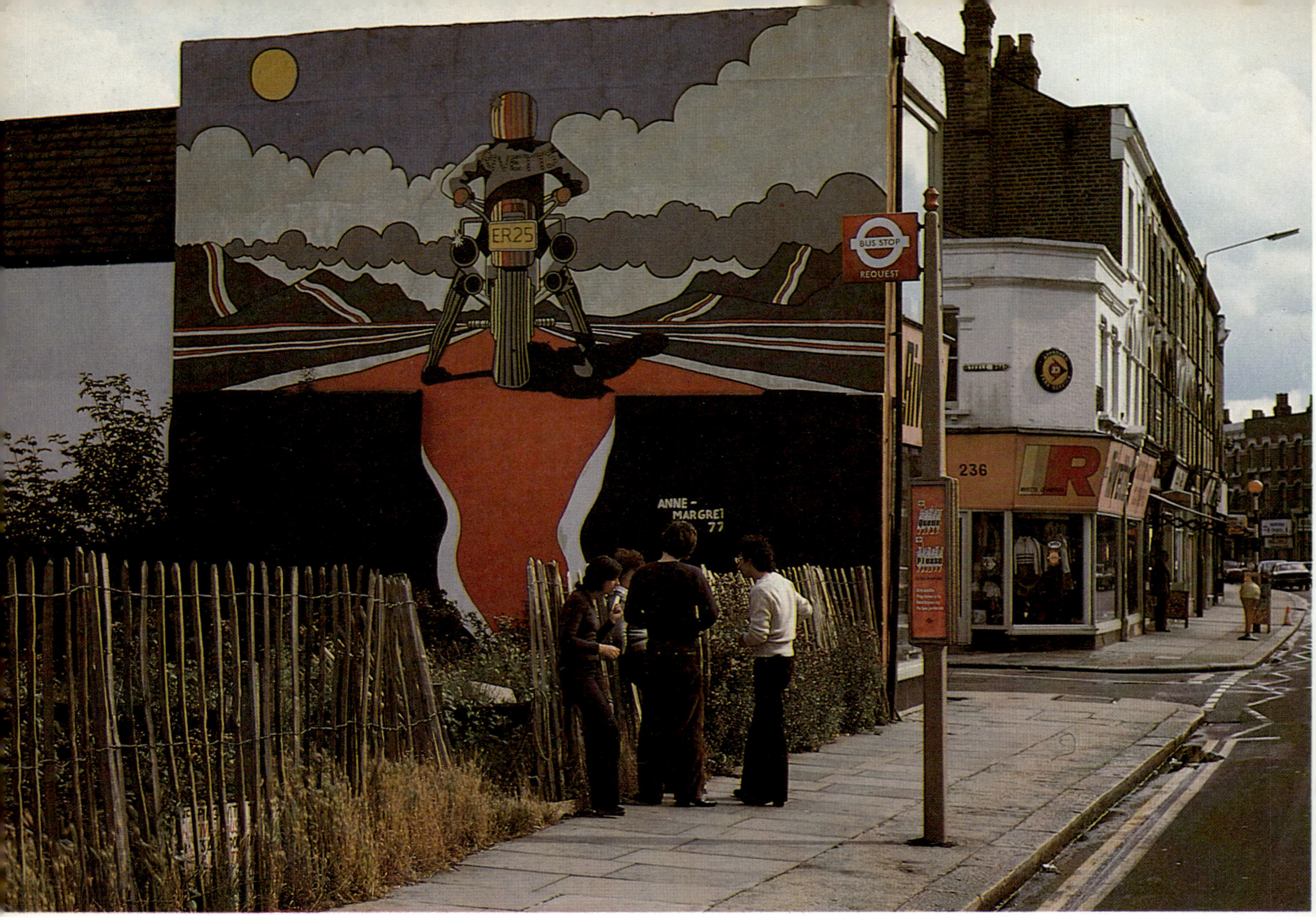

This mural in High Road, Leyton, London, was organized by the local council in order to improve the site. It also serves to advertise the motorcycle outfitters on to whose wall it is painted.

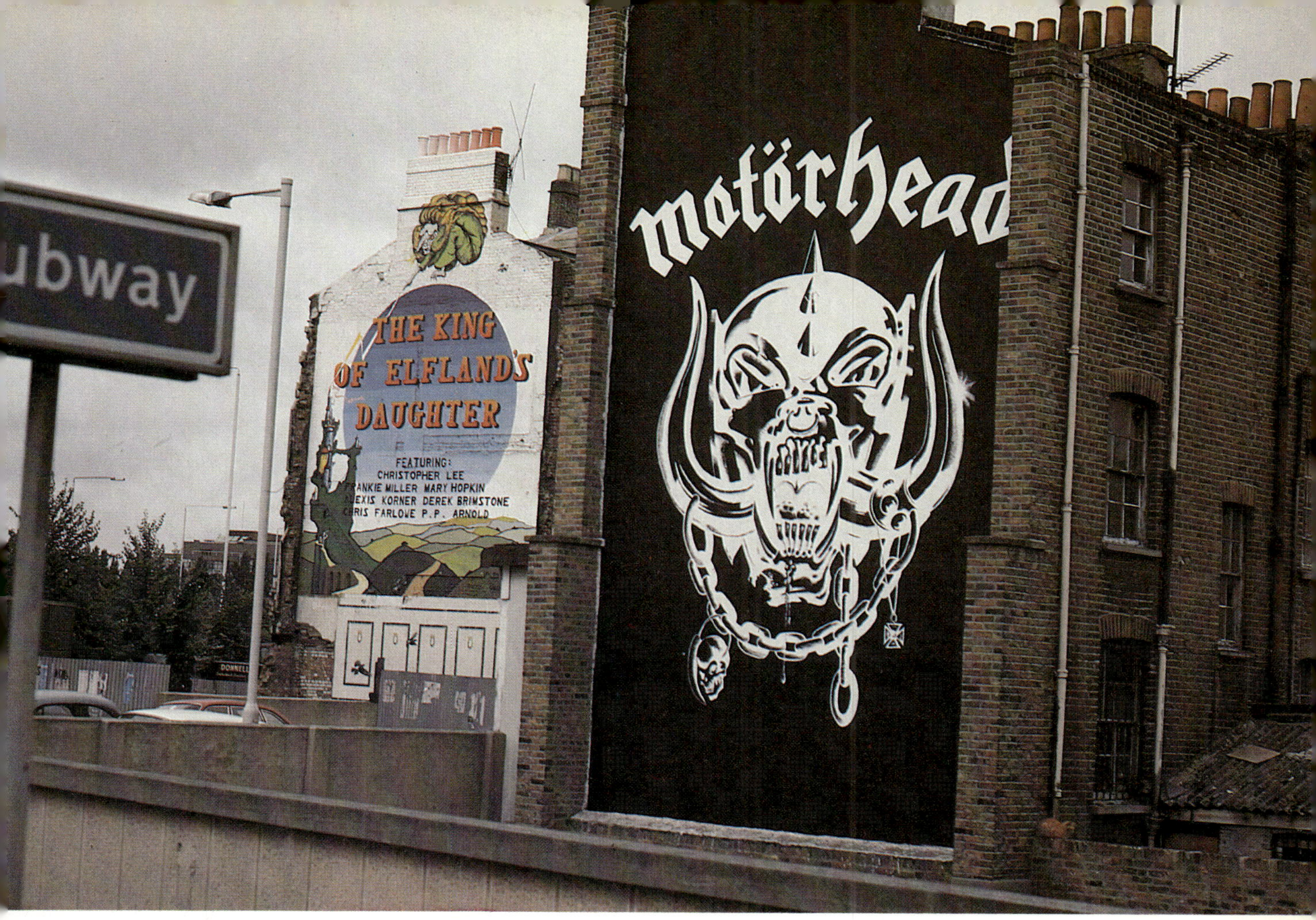

These two pop group advertisements were located at the busy Shepherd's Bush roundabout, London, and were a relatively inexpensive way of obtaining publicity.

London, Fulham, 18 Parsons Green Lane
Landscape on back party wall by J. McGuigan

London, Gospel Oak
Lismore Circus mural by the Fine Heart Squad

London, Greenwich, Creek Road
Albany mural by John Upton

London, Greenwich, Creek Road
The People's River by the Greenwich Mural Workshop (Stephen Lobb and Carol Kenna)

London, Islington, Churchill Railway foot-bridge (Tufnell Park)
Landscape decoration by pupils from Acland Burleigh School

London, Islington, Laycock School
Large murals by Dave Cashman, Roger Fagin and children

London, New Cross, Evelyn Estate
Extensive mural decorations outside and inside by 395 Group

London, Newham, Dames Road
Publicizing Newham Alternative Project by Anne-Margret Bellavoine

London, Royal Oak, under Westway
Two murals in honour of the working people of Paddington by Desmond Rochford and Dave Binnington

London, Royal Oak, under Westway, Portobello Road
Large figure and various decorations by Emily Young

London, Shepherd's Bush, Holland Park Avenue roundabout
Pop music advertisements by students from Chelsea Art School

London, Shepherd's Bush, Waldo Road
Country and townscape by Robin Collingwood

London, Shepherd's Bush, Thornfield Road
Exotic beach scene by the Fine Heart Squad

London, Shepherd's Bush, White City Road
Montage of popular images and people by Russel Barret

London, Southwark, Porlock Street
Ascension mural by Peter Petz

London, Swiss Cottage, Winchester Road
Mandala and Planet Landscape by the Fine Heart Squad

London, Tower Hamlets, Buxton Street, Robert Montefiore Infants School
Man and Dog Visiting Mars by Anne-Margret Bellavoine

London, Tower Hamlets, East India Dock Road and Portree Street
Scottish subjects and scenes by teachers and children from nearby schools

London, Tower Hamlets, Ben Johnson School, Hartford Street
Landscape murals in playground by all the children of the school

London, West Hampstead, Mill Lane
Railway wall by Liberation Films and local residents

London, Whitfield Street, Pollocks Toy Museum
Decoration

Londonderry, Bogside Hotel
Easter 1916—Tricolour Flag

Londonderry, Foyle Street
Brief Encounter by Noel Millar

Londonderry, Fountain Street
William of Orange by Bobbie Jackson

Manchester, All Saints, Oxford Road
Tiger in the Jungle by Glen Burton

Manchester, All Saints, North Western Museum of Science and Industry
Machinery found inside museum designed by Ken Billyard and painted by Walter Kershaw

Manchester, Denton
Decorated barber's shop by David Vaughan

Manchester, Heywood (Manchester Road)
Alvin Stardust by Walter Kershaw, Eric Kean and Paul O'Reilly

Manchester, Hulme Centre, near Library
Beach scene and other decorations

Manchester, Moston, Hollinwood Avenue
Painted holiday advertisements by Walter Kershaw

Manchester, Walkden, Alexander Road
Anne Hathaway's cottage

Manchester, West Gorton, Hyde Road
Pictorial descriptions of industrial complex by David Vaughan

Midlothian, Currie, 9 Nethercurrie Crescent
Painted garage door by Gillian Waugh

Milton Keynes, Netherfield
Giraffe by Liz Leyh

Milton Keynes, Galley Hill Underpasses, Stantonbury, Greenleys
Painted underpasses by John Czaky

Mitcham, Surrey, Watermeads Estate
Local history design by Graham Cooper

Isle of Mull, Lochdon
Murinals, a highlander (Gents) and a mermaid (Ladies) by Lionel Leslie

Newcastle upon Tyne, Byker
Balloon motif painted onto architect's site office

Newcastle upon Tyne, Byker
Spaceman walking by Duncan Newton

Newcastle upon Tyne, Gosforth, 41 Church Road
Gypsy-styled front door by Scott-Dobson

Newcastle upon Tyne, Jesmond, Gladstone Terrace
Bird of Paradise in the Jungle by Tricia Gilman

New Malden, 125 Elm Road
Large Islamic carpet by David Whitaker

Norwich, Sprowden Road, Prince of Denmark
Painted relief of man on a white charger

Oldham, Condor factory
Condor commercial by Walter Kershaw

Plymouth, Barbican, The Parade
Assembly of Elizabethan characters and philosophers by Robert Lenkiewicz

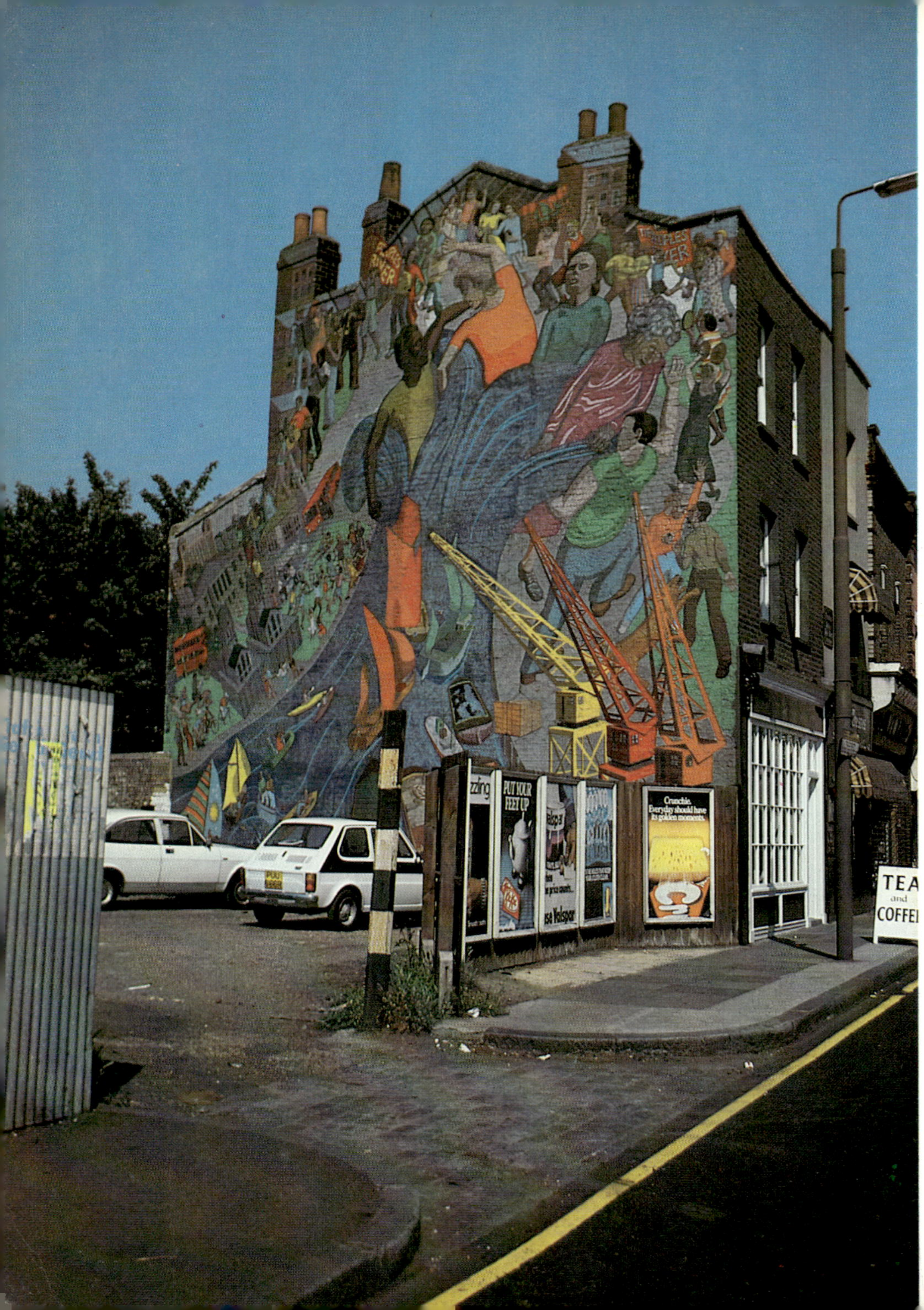

Stephen Lobb and Carol Kenna of the Greenwich Mural Workshop have a policy of collaborating with local communities to establish suitable designs. Their approach is based on the manual produced by the Chicago Public Art Workshop, which states that a prerequisite for success is the artist's readiness to respond to the suggestions of the local people.

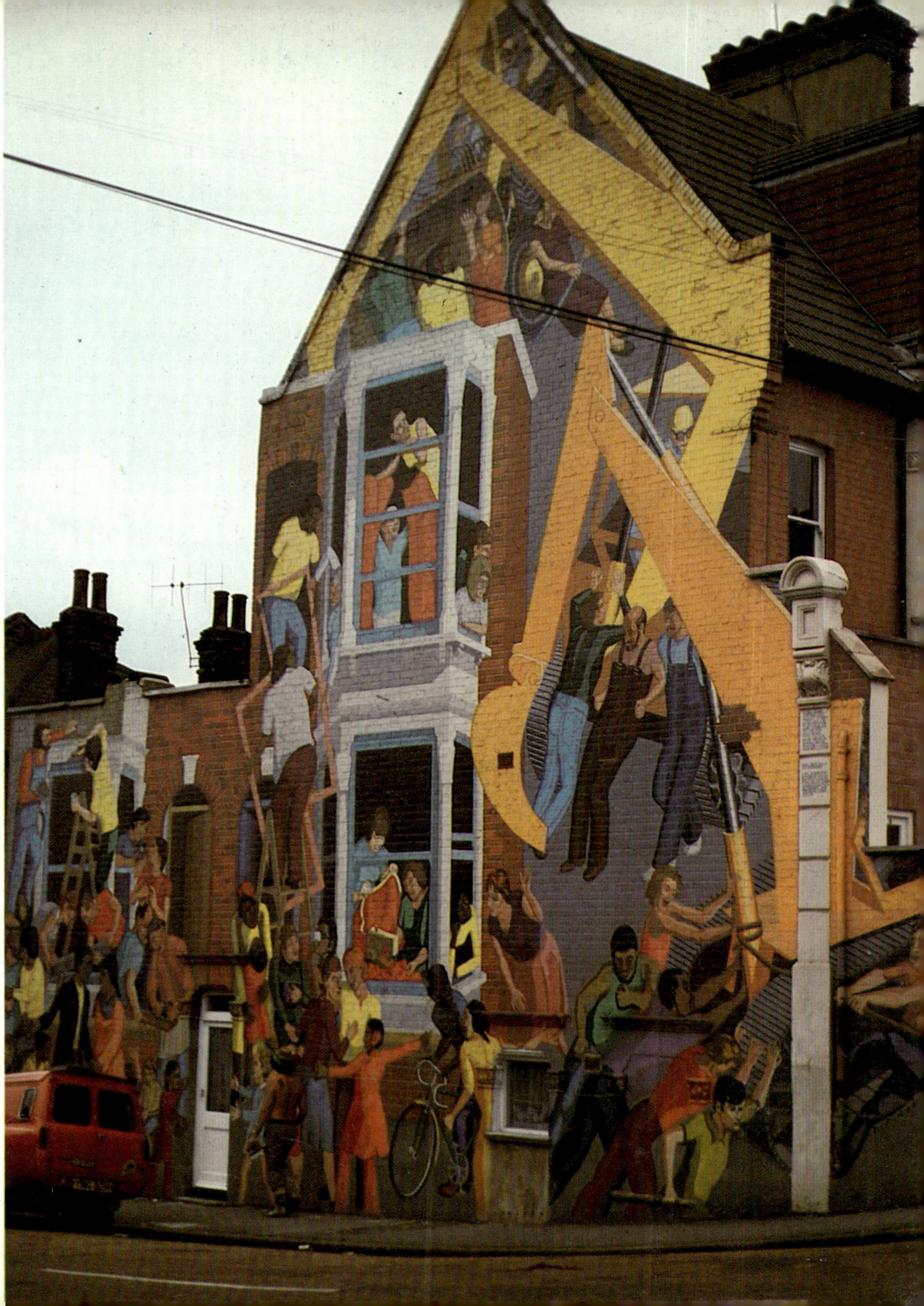

As Floyd Road in Charlton was threatened by demolition, its inhabitants called upon the Greenwich Mural Workshop to express their opposition. The painting depicts the local people resisting the bulldozers and repairing their houses.

Porth, Abberhondda Road
Miners 'ura mural' by Alan Warburton and pupils from local comprehensive schools

Porth, Pontyprydd Road
Daffodils 'ura mural' by Alan Warburton

Quorn, near Loughborough, Hurst Hotel
Painted relief of Art Nouveau-type lady

Rochdale, Derby Street
Lancashire house interior by Walter Kershaw

Rochdale, Edward Street
Chinese Dragon by Walter Kershaw and Linda Hulse

Rochdale, Entwistle Road
Pansies by Walter Kershaw

Rochdale, Halifax Road
Water Temple by Linda Gamer, Walter Kershaw and Eric Kean

Rochdale, Littleborough, Cote Lane
Pennine landscape by Walter Kershaw, Eric Kean, Paul O'Reilly and Graham Cooper

Runcorn, Portland Street
Narrowboats on surrounding canals by Pete McFerran and students

Sheffield, opposite Cubicle Theatre
Preposed art into landscape mural

Sterling, Station Underpass
Subway designs based on graffiti by local children

Sunderland, Moor Court
Old seamen's general store by Ken Watts

Swindon, Fleming Way
Golden Lion Canal bridge by Ken White and Thamesdown Community Arts Project

Swindon, Manton Road
Uccello's George and the Dragon by pupils from the local school

Swindon, Westcote Road
Bavarian castle landscape by the Thamesdown Community Arts Project

Swindon, Town Centre
Railway Village, express train passing the local railway works by the Thamesdown Community Arts Project

Swindon, Penhill
Old bridge of Castle Coombe by a local scout troop and Thamesdown Community Arts Project

Upton, Youth Club, Yorkshire
Montage of the local scene

Wallsend, Northairdes Road
Local scene with references to shipbuilding by Duncan Newton and local residents

Wigan, Higher Ince, Taylors Lane
The Oasis by David Vaughan

Widnes, Old Market
Old bridges and the river Mersey by Alun Evans and students

This is a list of the most ambitious murals up until 1978. However, owing to the great number of murals, not all examples are included in this list.

Overleaf

above: This good, bad, and ugly interpretation of Battersea took the Wandsworth Mural Workshop two years to complete. The leader of the group, Brian Barnes, maintains that community involvement and the actual process of painting is as important as the finished product.

below: This design on the boundary wall of the new Watermeads Estate in Mitcham, Surrey, alludes to the history and features of the area. The interwinding grid-type pattern linking the various components reflects the architect's original intention of designing a housing estate that respects the existing landscape.

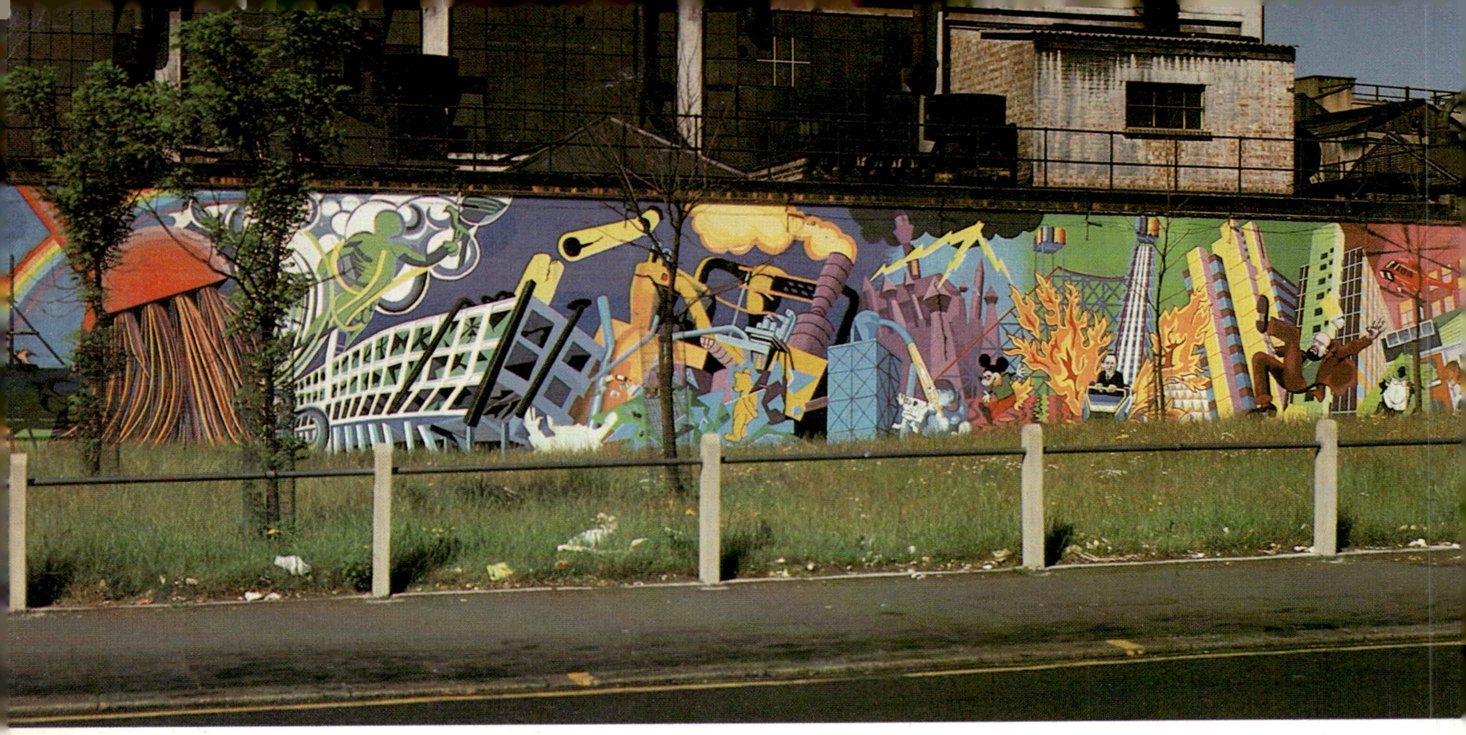

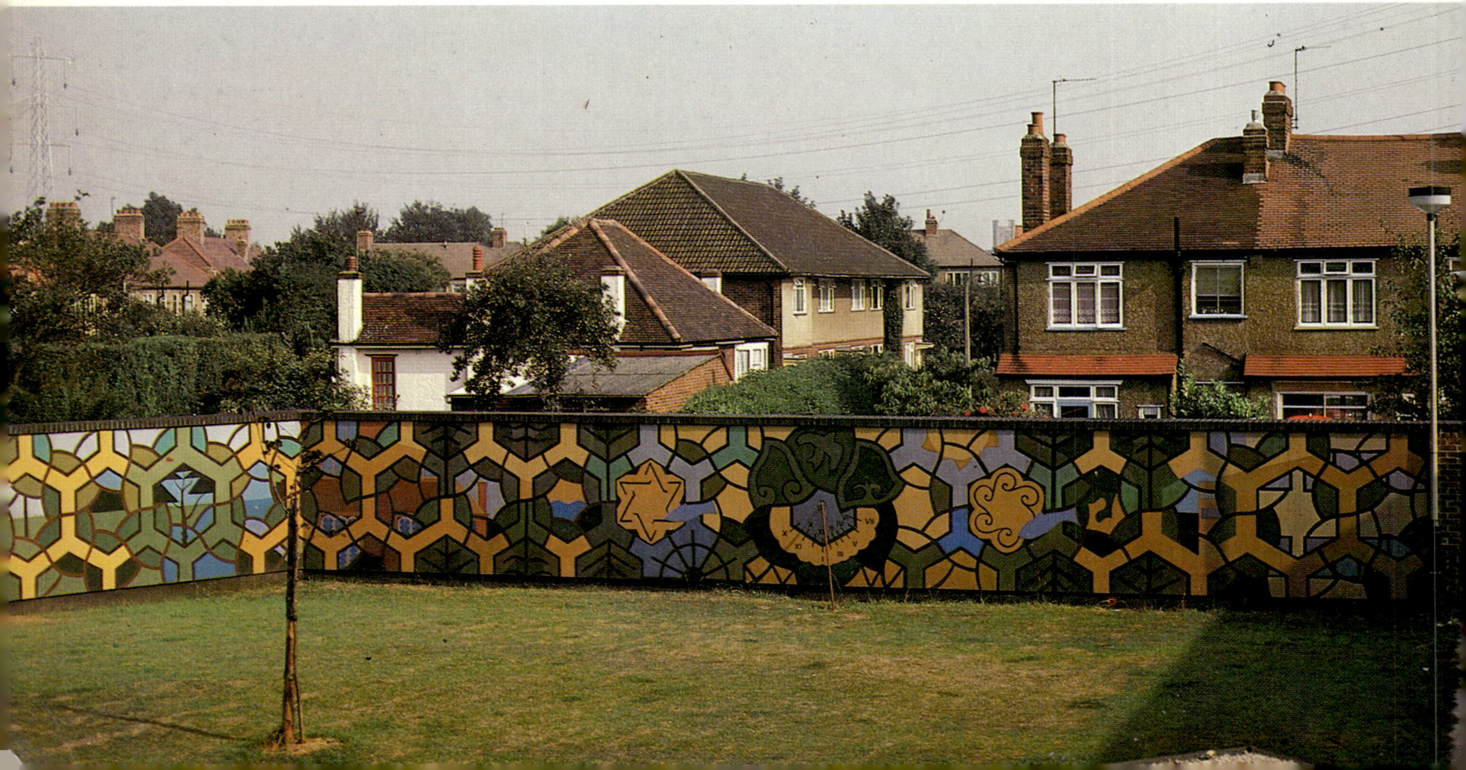

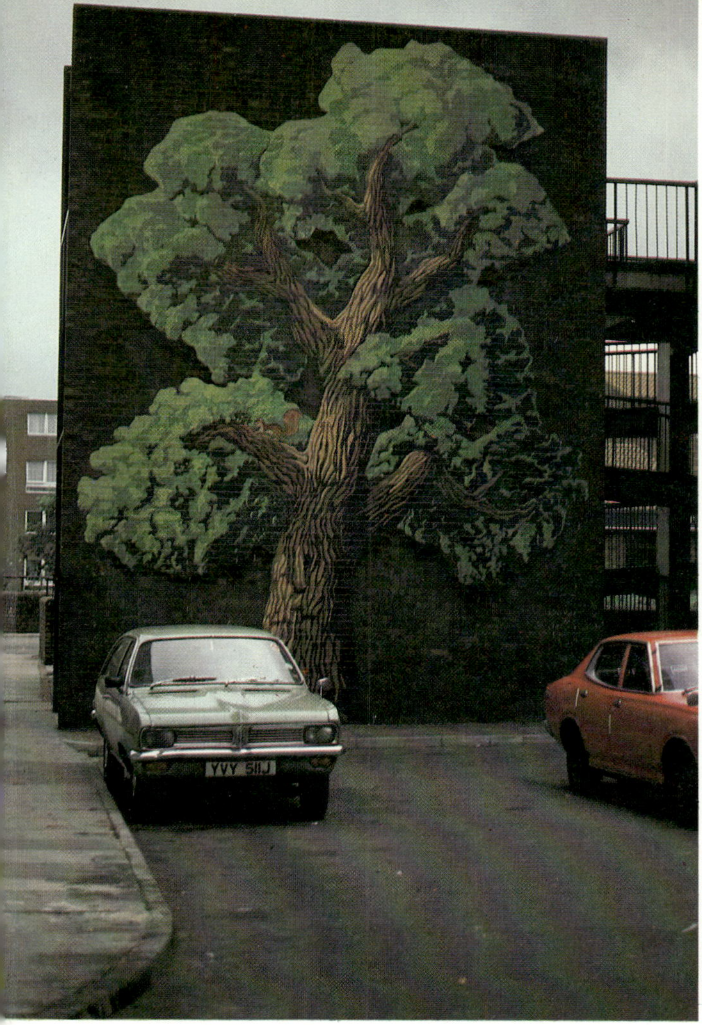

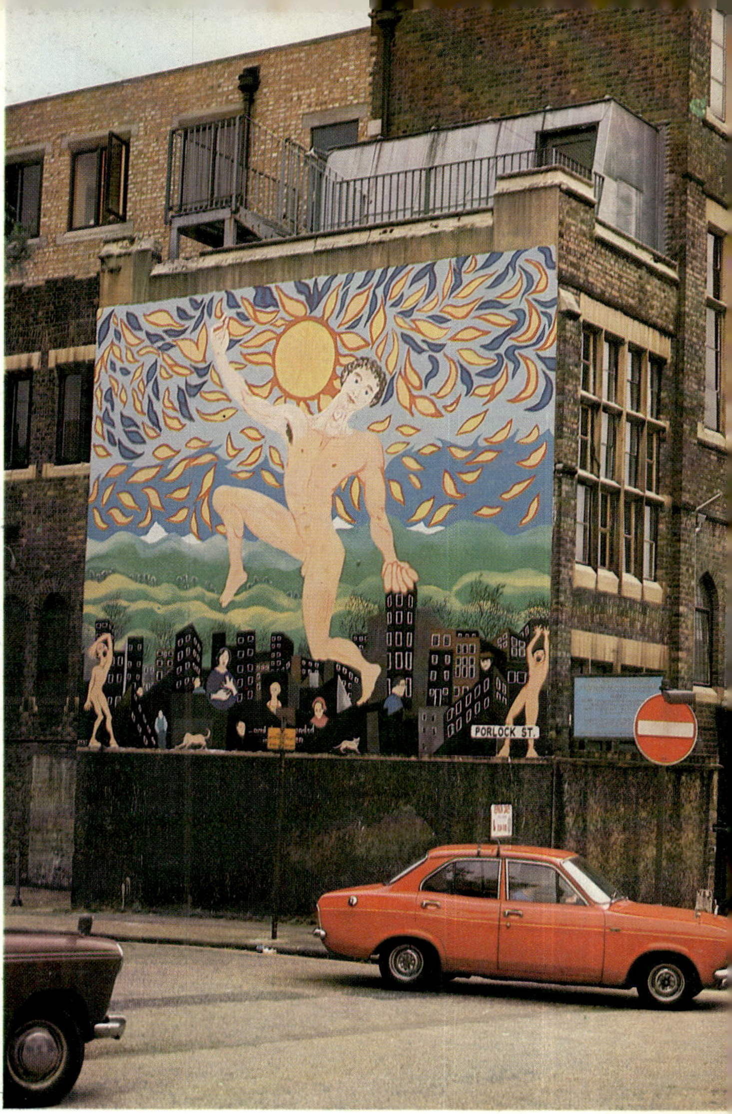

left: This tree image on the Evelyn Estate, London, was part of an extensive project that was undertaken in 1976-7 by the 395 Group. The project was created in order to introduce some colour and imagination into an otherwise impersonal environment. The themes were suggested by the residents, approved by the Lewisham Council, and elaborated by the Group.

right: The Ascension mural in Porlock Street is one of Peter Petz' many church paintings around London. The artist believes his murals should be located where they fulfil a purpose.